knits

to share and care

GERARD ALLT

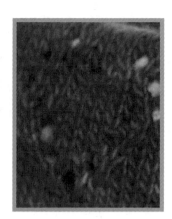

knits
to share and care

D&C
David and Charles

www.mycraftivity.com

Dedicated to Louis and James

David and Charles

A DAVID & CHARLES BOOK

David & Charles is an F+W Publications Inc. company
4700 East Galbraith Road
Cincinnati, OH 45236

First published in the UK in 2008
By David & Charles Publishers
Brunel House, Newton Abbot
Devon TQ12 4PU

2 4 6 8 10 9 7 5 3 1

A CIP catalogue record for this book
is available from the British Library.

ISBN-13: 978-0-7153-3015-9
ISBN-10: 0-7153-3015-2

Printed in Malaysia
for David & Charles
Brunel House   Newton Abbot   Devon
Visit our website at **www.davidandcharles.co.uk**

David & Charles books are available from all good bookshops;
alternatively you can contact our Orderline on 0870 9908222
or write to us at FREEPOST EX2 110, D&C Direct, Newton Abbot,
TQ12 4ZZ (no stamp required UK only); US customers
call 800-289-0963 and Canadian customers call 800-840-5220.

For Fil Rouge Press

Publisher Judith More
Art Director Sharon Spencer
Senior Editor Jo Godfrey Wood
Editor Amanda Burfoot
Editorial Assistant Hannah Sergeant
Production Director Kate MacPhee
Photographer Robin Lever
Illustrator Zoe Austin
Chart Designer Cindy Moore

Contents

Introduction

There are many knitting stereotypes, some true, some false. One of the most common is that hand-knitting is a solitary exercise, practised by lonely spinsters behind closed doors. I have always seen hand-knitting as the opposite to this, as a very social enterprise; a perfect, portable activity, ideal for the pub, the park or a journey. There have been so many times in my life when the boredom of waiting for a train or a plane has been alleviated by having my knitting bag to hand!

Through my knitting group, I Knit London, I have met such a huge number of knitters who share a passion for the craft and who have shared with me, and with others, tips, skills, ideas and inspiration. When we started over two years ago it was an excuse for get-togethers with other like-minded people, to have a few drinks, a laugh and a gossip. Now our weekly meetings are a regular place to catch up with friends and to make new ones.

KNITTING TO SHARE AND CARE

One constant topic of conversation at our meetings is the amount of knitting that we do for other people – whether it's a new baby, an old friend, someone who has done something special, or simply someone you love. The stories we've shared have been inspirational, emotional, funny and some just plain weird – but everyone has their own experience and their own moments to share. This book is inspired by some of their stories – there are projects here for all knitters, whether you've just learned to cast on, or whether you've been a lifelong knitter.

My early experiences as a knitter were full of joy and positive emotions as I usually knitted things for my friends' babies. Since I no longer lived near most of my friends who were becoming new parents, learning to knit by making them baby clothes was brilliant as it meant that I felt much more connected to what was happening to them, to how their lives were changing.

The patterns in this book are designed to be knitted and shared with others; those who have been there for you during difficult times; those who need a lift; those who have shared; those have cared – from small tokens to great gifts. They are special projects for special people.

I sincerely hope that you'll enjoy knitting them as much as we have enjoyed putting them together.

For those you love

This book is full of patterns to knit things for the people that you love. I have always found knitting to be a great way to show people I love them. One of the things I value most in my friends is their time. There are a million ways to spend your time and the fact that someone chooses to spend it with me shows me that they love me. I have lots of friends who live in different parts of the country, some in different countries, and I like to send them knitted things.

In this caring collection you will find designs that are particularly appropriate for life changes, such as pregnancy or a new baby, or particular needs such as a scratch-free sweater for a child with a skin allergy or a belt for someone with back pain. Not everything I make to send is serious or for a particular occasion, and I like the fact that I can simply just think of the people I love and remember them while I am knitting. Friends are important and should be cherished.

For those in need

There are people in need all over the world. Later in the book you will find lots of links to various ways of helping some of those people through your knitting. There is a long tradition of knitting to help other people. From hats to gloves, socks and blankets, your knitting will help someone out of poverty or support them through a time of crisis. The bond of community strengthened through knitting means a great deal to me. I hope that you will be inspired by the contents of this book.

KNITTING THAT CARES FOR OTHERS

Throughout history, knitters have responded generously to those in need – from bonnets for Victorian orphans, through socks for soldiers in both world wars, to blankets for disaster relief appeals. Today, many knitting circles get together to craft for charity. When your family and friends already have ample love and gifts, reaching out with your needles and yarn to needy strangers is a satisfying way to practise your craft. For further advice and information on charity knitting see pages 134-5.

The WaterAid River

Knit A River was a campaign to raise awareness of the 1.1 billion people without access to safe water.

Between May 2006 and July 2007 I Knit joined with WaterAid to mobilise knitters across the globe to create the world's first knitted petition – a huge river of knitted blue squares.

The purpose of the project was to inspire enough people to take action and help WaterAid apply public pressure on governments and decision-makers to ensure they did all that was possible to improve the lives of the billions of people who do not have access to safe drinking water. Another outcome was an amazing knitted river, or 'knitition', which WaterAid could show off at events as a means to grab public attention and to engage people with their vital work.

Thanks to the many people who volunteered to sew these tiny squares together, the river has been used at a number of events since 2006 to support WaterAid campaign's team and their work, always attracting attention!

On Saturday 14th July 2007 the largest part of the river to be shown so far appeared draped like a waterfall from the roof of the National Theatre on London's South Bank. Part of the theatre's annual Watch This Space festival, WaterAid volunteers engaged with passers-by, presenting them with information on the End Water Poverty campaign. It was a spectacular sight!

The river has also been seen at shows across the UK and abroad, including the Dutch Stitch 'n Bitch Day in Rotterdam (2006), Unravel at Bracknell (2006), Jubilee Gardens in London (2006), the Knitting and Stitching Show at Alexandra Palace (2007), the UK Stitch 'n Bitch Day (2007) and many others. Parts of the river will continue to be used to promote WaterAid at future events.

The river's finest hour came in May 2007 when, just ahead of the G8 summit in Germany, over 300 knitters, WaterAid staff and supporters carried swathes of the knitted river, almost 500 metres in length, along Albert Embankment, across Lambeth Bridge and into Parliament Square and Whitehall, the home of the British Government. The culmination of the march was the presentation of a section of the knitted petition to the Prime Minister at 10 Downing Street. Marching with the knitted river we demanded that the G8 do more to end water poverty.

The 'Knit a River' project is possibly the largest knitting project ever undertaken, with thousands of knitters and stitchers equally responsible for this incredible work of art.

WaterAid is an international non-governmental organisation (NGO). Their mission is to overcome poverty by enabling the world's poorest people to gain access to safe water, sanitation and hygiene education. They work with local communities in 17 countries in Africa and Asia.

To find out more about getting involved with WaterAid visit **www.wateraid.org**

KNITTING THAT CARES FOR THE EARTH

As concern for the planet increases, so do the many ways in which we, as knitters, can help to limit the effects we have on the world. We can reuse and recycle; rip out old knitted items and reuse the yarns. We can mend, repair and reclaim; we're crafty; you know what I'm talking about!

More and more yarn producers are moving to organic practices. Included in this book are two patterns using fantastic organic yarns from the British Isles: Garthenor and Cornish Organic. Both yarns are very special and I've used them for a number of my own projects – they come highly recommended by me.

But you don't need to use organic yarns to make a difference – there are choices to be made at all stages of your knitting project. Another personal favourite of mine is yarn that is produced by companies like the Natural Dye Studio, who create the most beautiful range of colours using natural, chemical-free dyes. For home spinners and dyers there is now a wide range of natural dyes available. Your choice of needles is almost as wide as the choice of yarns – many knitters now eschew the traditional plastic and aluminium needles in favour of more comfortable and ethically sourced wooden and bamboo sets. From a personal point of view, I prefer the smooth birchwood needles from Brittany, made using wood from sustainable Californian birch. For an extra-special treat I upgrade to the exquisite Lantern Moon needles – made from a selection of woods: ebony, coconut palm, blonde wood and rosewood. These needles are produced by a group of Vietnamese craftsmen and women using traditional methods and are sold throughout the world.

The Great British Sheep

We love British yarn! American yarns are very sought-after at the moment and we wanted to take a bit of time to shout about all the amazing breeds of sheep native to the UK and all the wonderful yarn producers we have on our doorstep. Whilst it's hard to resist some of the stuff you can get from overseas, from Japanese silk with a stainless-steel core from Habu, to the ultimate luxury qiviut from the wild arctic musk ox, I always like to use British wool for regular projects, often substituting yarn if possible. Not only does this support local businesses up and down the country, it gives directly to the farmers and yarn producers. Of course, one obvious benefit of using home-grown yarns is the reduction in the carbon footprint – many yarns, unfortunately, do have to travel the globe to reach your local yarn store.

Great Britain has an incredible tradition of wool production, from clipping to spinning, dying and knitting, and we are in danger of losing this. The Great British Sheep is a project we started in 2008 to collect yarns from all 60 breeds of British sheep. Our giant sheep sculpture will be covered in a unique 'knitted fleece' made by members of the public. The yarns are from all over the country; our intention is to show knitters that British wool is as disparate and as exciting as the country itself. Each yarn has its own qualities and character and we aim to show the possibilities of using wool from the British Isles.

Bounty for Babies & Toddlers

A BLANKET OF LOVE
Angelic hearts for a special new-born

GIVE THEM A PRAYER SHAWL
Delicate lace wrap for every generation

BABY'S COMING HOME
Welcoming outfit for a premature baby

BOUNTIFUL BOOTEES
Stash-busting first coverings for bare feet

ROSEMARY (OR ROBERT) RABBIT
An organic wool toy for a child to care for

SCRATCH-FREE SWEATER
Softest alpaca cable knit for sensitive skin

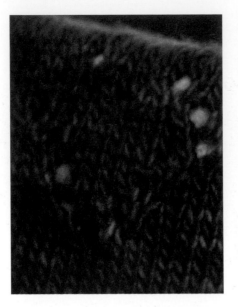

A BLANKET OF LOVE
Angelic hearts for a special new-born
by Gerard Allt

Everyone needs a blanket full of love. I designed this one for my new nephews, 6-month-old Louis and then-unborn James. They were both long-awaited so there was extra love when they arrived, if that is possible! They both have one, and it has become their favourite blanket.

I chose a simple lace heart design so as not to trap their delicate little fingers, and kept the size relatively small. The blanket is perfect for the cot, the pram or even to wrap your baby in to protect them from the chills in the air. The colour is important – for me it could only be red, the colour of love, though your blanket should be your colour of choice.

MATERIALS

Yarn
2 hanks of Manos Del Uruguay Silk Blend, shade 6461

Needles
1 pair 4.5 mm needles

TENSION
22 sts and 30 rows over 10 cm (4 ins)

SIZE
Length: 86 cm (34 ins)
Width: 45 cm (17³/₄ ins)

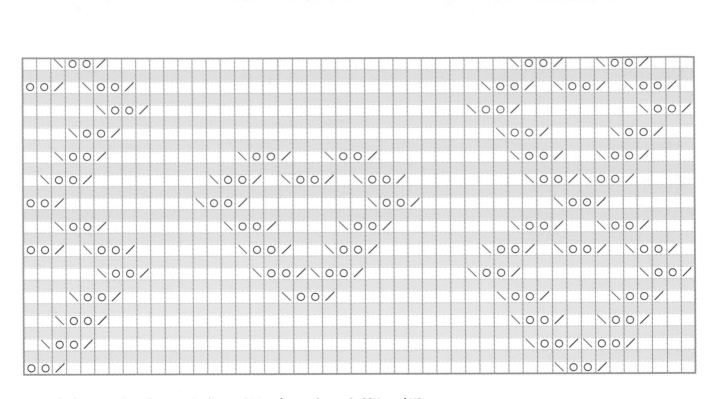

KEY: Blank row: Knit Lilac row: Purl ⭘ Yarn forward ⟍ SSK ⟋ K2 tog

HINTS AND TIPS

- You could use any double-knit yarn – for example, a machine-washable wool such as Emu superwash DK. With a different yarn you may need to adjust the needle size.

- The pattern is easily adjustable: just vary the number of stitches and/or rows, but make sure you place the heart lace panel in the middle.

- If you need to start a new ball, join the yarn a few stitches in from the edge, rather than on the edge of the shawl, and it will be easier to weave in the ends and keep a neat edge.

- Garter stitch is a little smaller than stocking stitch, so extra vigilance when blocking is called for. You could use a moss stitch border if you prefer.

ABBREVIATIONS
K knit
P purl
St(s) stitch(es)
SSK Slip, slip, knit
K2 tog knit two together

KNITTING THE BLANKET
Cast on 160 sts.
Knit 10 rows in garter stitch.
Next Row: K.
Next Row: K12, p to last 12 sts, k12.
Repeat these 2 rows 19 times.

Working the Heart Pattern
Keeping the 12 sts garter-stitch border at either side, follow the pattern chart, working in stocking stitch.

Next Row: K.
Next Row: K12, p to last 12 sts, k12.
Repeat these 2 rows 19 times.
Knit 10 rows in garter stitch.
Cast off.

Finishing
Neatly weave in any loose ends.

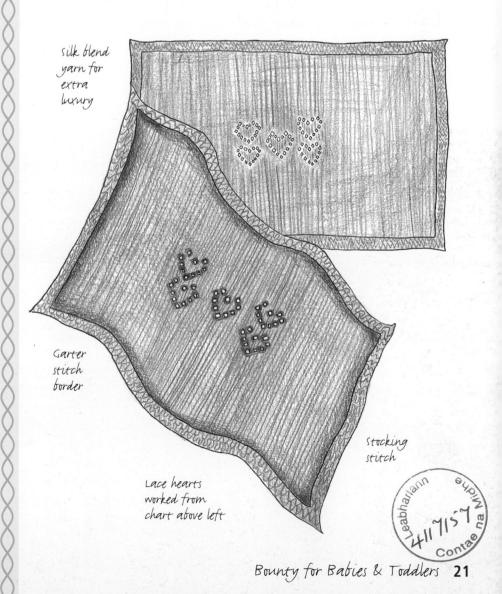

silk blend yarn for extra luxury

Garter stitch border

stocking stitch

Lace hearts worked from chart above left

GIVE THEM A PRAYER SHAWL
Delicate lace wrap for every generation
by Gerard Allt

This wonderful shawl was designed with my grandmother, Mary Catherine McHale, in mind. In her home town of Liverpool, in the first half of the 20th century, she was a constant shawl wearer, especially when she attended Mass. A prayer shawl like this could provide her with dignity, allow her to express her faith and also add some much-needed extra warmth in a chilly church. Of course, such shawls were made for new babies, too, becoming a special gift of love to celebrate the long-awaited babe's arrival.

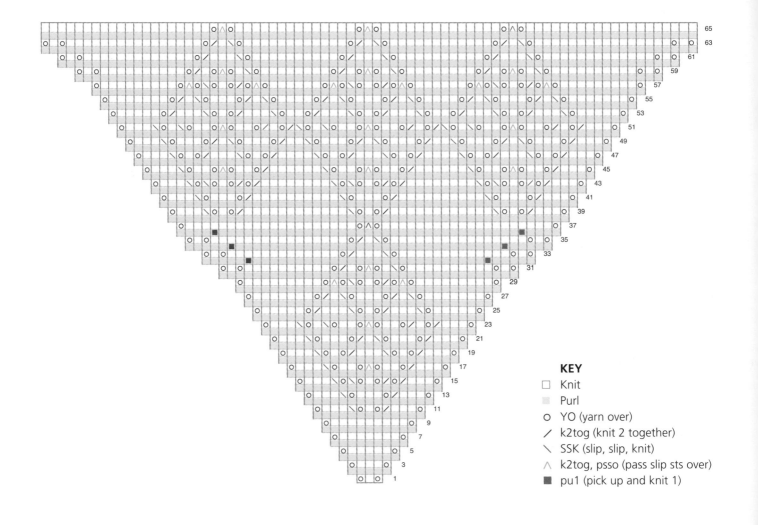

KEY

□	Knit
▪	Purl
○	YO (yarn over)
╱	k2tog (knit 2 together)
╲	SSK (slip, slip, knit)
∧	k2tog, psso (pass slip sts over)
■	pu1 (pick up and knit 1)

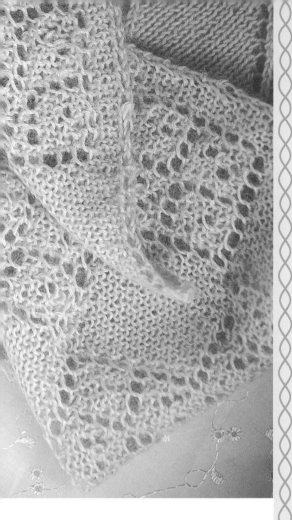

HINTS AND TIPS

- Knitted lace is not as difficult as you might think. However, as lace designs are often worked in fine yarn they can take time, which is why a small piece like this is perfect for a first attempt at lace knitting.

- This shawl can serve for grown-up dressy occasions, too. It would make a glamorous evening accessory worked in yarns such as Rowan Kidsilk Haze or Tilli Tomas Beaded lace silk yarn.

- This ethereal lacy wrap could also give comfort to parents who have lost a baby – either as a still-birth or early in life. They can wrap the baby in the shawl to say goodbye, then keep it with their pictures in a memory box. A list of charities that collect items to give to grieving parents can be found on page 134.

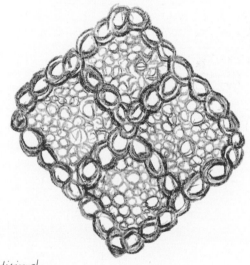

Traditional
diamond lace
pattern

MATERIALS

Yarn
1 x 50 g Wensleydale longwool 4-ply yarn in cream, shade 601

NEEDLES
1 pair 2.5 mm needles

TENSION
9 sts and 14 rows over 4 cm (1½ ins)

KNITTING THE SHAWL
Cast on 5 stitches.

Work the diamond lace pattern, following the chart on the left, and purling alternate rows (the lilac squares on the chart), until you have 90 sts.

Cast off.

BABY'S COMING HOME
Welcoming outfit for a premature baby
by Just Call Me Ruby

My sister, Maxine, was premature and my mum sometimes tells stories of Maxine's time in an incubator and about her fears when she was born. Many of our customers come into the shop with stories about how hard it is to find patterns for premature baby clothes. So this book had to have a 'coming home' outfit. I also knew that Ruby would be the perfect person to design it, as her daughter, Charlotte, was born 10 weeks early and weighed in at only just over 0.5 kg (2 lbs).

Ruby told me: 'Her lungs couldn't work for themselves and she was given 24 hours to live. Somehow, thanks to the dedication of her doctors and nurses and her own will to live, she survived, and 9 weeks later, now weighing around 2 kg (5 lbs), we were allowed to take her home. We looked everywhere for clothes to dress her in to bring her home. There was nothing. In the end she came home wearing a doll's pram suit bought from a toy store. Things have improved a lot since then, but a lot of the patterns on offer are aimed at the premature baby while in hospital, and I wanted to knit the outfit I would have loved my little girl to have come home in.'

MATERIALS

Yarn
3 x 50 g balls Rowan Fine Milk Cotton in Barley Sugar 481

Needles
1 x 2.5 mm circular needle
1 pair 2.5 mm straight needles
1 set of 2.5 mm double-pointed needles
1 x 2 mm crochet hook

Other Materials
Shirring elastic (optional)

SIZE
To fit a 4–5 lb (1.8–2.3 kg) baby

TENSION
11 sts and 16 rows over 4 cm (1½ ins)

ABBREVIATIONS
K knit
P purl
St(s) stitch(es)
WS wrong side
RS right side
SKPO slip 1, knit 1, pass the slipped stitch over
Inc increase(ing)
M1 make 1 stitch
DPNS double-pointed needles
SSK slip, slip, knit (see Glossary for details)
SM slip marker
W&T wrap and turn (see Glossary for details)

GLOSSARY
SSK slip 2 sts, insert left needle into front loop of slipped st, k together through the back loops

W&T on a RS row, bring yarn to front of work between needles, sl next st onto right-hand needle, bring yarn round this st to back of work, sl st back onto left-hand needle, turn; on a WS row, bring yarn to back of work between needles, sl next st onto right-hand needle, bring yarn around st to front of work, st st back onto left-hand needle, turn

Knitting the Hat
Using 2.5 mm dpns, cast on 78 sts.

Join into round, placing marker at join.

Work 3 rounds in moss stitch.

Next Round: P.

Next Round: K1 (p11, k2) 5 times, p11, k1.

Next Round: K2 (p9, k4) 5 times, p9, k2.

Continue in this manner, working triangles as for jacket.

Work 27 rounds without shaping.

Shaping the Crown
Next Round: K7, k2tog (k8, k2tog) 6 times, k7, k2tog.

Next Round: K6, k2tog (k7, k2tog) 6 times, k6, k2tog.

Continue in this manner, reducing number of stitches between decreases on each round, until 6 sts remain.

Draw thread through remaining sts.

Fasten off.

Finishing
Darn in ends.
Press lightly through damp cloth.

Knitting the Jacket
Knitting the Body
Using a 2.5 mm circular needle, cast on 138 sts.
1st Row: (K1, p1) repeat to end of row. Repeat this row twice more.

Working the Triangle Pattern
Next Row: (WS) (k1, p1) twice, k to last 4 sts (k1, p1) twice.

Next Row: (P1, k1) twice (p11, k2) 9 times, p11, k1 (p1, k1) twice.

Next Row: (K1, p1) twice, p2 (k9, p4) 9 times, k9, p2 (k1, p1) twice.

Next Row: (P1, k1) twice, k3 (p7, k6)

9 times, p7, k3 (p1, k1) twice.

Next Row: (K1, p1) twice, p4 (k5, p8) 9 times, k5, p4 (k1, p1) twice.

Next Row: (P1, k1) twice, k5 (p3, k10) 9 times, p3, k5 (p1, k1) twice.

Next Row: (K1, p1) twice, p6 (k1, p12) 9 times, k1, p6 (k1, p1) twice.

Next Row: (P1, k1) twice, k to last 4sts, placing stitch markers immediately above 'point' of 3rd and 8th triangles (p1, k1) twice.

Continue working moss stitch border as set, but now proceed working centre section in stocking stitch.

Work decreases on 5th and every following 4th round 4 times at markers until 118 sts remain as follows:

SKPO, place st back onto left-hand needle point and slip next st on that needle over this stitch, return st to right-hand needle point and continue in stocking stitch to next marker. Repeat.

Work one p row.

Transfer remaining sts to a spare circular needle.

Knitting the Sleeves (make 2)
Using 2.5 mm dpns, cast on 30 sts.

Divide these sts evenly between 3 needles (10 sts per needle).

Join into round, placing marker at beginning of round.

Work 3 rounds in moss stitch.

Next Round: (RS) k, inc 3 sts evenly across round (33 sts).

Next Round: P.

Next Round: K1 (p9, k2) twice, p9, k1.

Next Round: K2 (p7, k4) twice, p7, k2.

Next Round: K3 (p5, k6) twice, p5, k3.

Next Round: K4 (p3, k8) twice, p3, k4.

Next Round: K5 (p1, k10) twice, p1, k5.

K all rounds from this point and m1 either side of marker on next and every following 3rd round 7 times (47 sts).

Work without further shaping for 10 rows.

Reposition sts on dpns, leaving 2 sts on either side of marker on a safety pin.

Knitting the Yoke
Note: At all times throughout the remainder of the pattern, maintain the 4-st moss stitch border on body fronts.

With RS of body facing, k to within 2 sts of 1st marker, place next 4 sts onto a safety pin.

With RS of sleeve facing, k sts on right sleeve (placing markers at either end of sleeve), k sts on back to within 2 sts of next marker, place next 4 sts onto another safety pin, k sts on left sleeve, again placing markers, k remaining sts on left front (212 sts).

Work yoke in stocking stitch in rows.

Work 1 row.

Next Row: (RS) m1 at each marker (216 sts).

Work 2 rows.

Work Triangle Pattern as for body but work 13 triangles instead of 10.

Shaping the Yoke
Working in stocking stitch, dec on next and 4 following alternate rows as follows: K to within 2 sts of marker, ssk, sm, k2tog, repeat at each marker, thereby decreasing 8 sts on each row until 184 sts remain, ending with a RS row.

Commence Neck Shaping
Next Row: P to last 10 sts, w&t, work to last 10 sts, w&t. Work on these 164 sts only.

Next Row: (WS) p2tog across row (82 sts).

Next Row: K2tog across row (41 sts).

Next Row: Without turning work, k across all sts to left front edge, turn and cast on 39 sts.

Cut off yarn and rejoin to right front edge with RS facing.

Cast on 40 sts (140 sts).

Work across all stitches in moss stitch.

Work a further 2 rows in moss stitch.

Cast off in pattern.

Knitting the Underarms
Using dpns, place the 4 sts on sleeve and corresponding underarm with right sides together. K together using 3-needle bind off.

Repeat on second sleeve.

Finishing
Darn in all ends. Press lightly through a damp cloth.

Knitting the Pants
(worked from the top down)

Working the Front
Using a 2.5 mm circular needle, cast on 100 sts.

Join into a round.

Work 6 rounds in k1, p1 rib.

K in the round until work measures 10 cm (4 ins) from cast-on edge.

Divide work evenly onto two straight needles (50 sts on each).

Working the Back
With RS facing, cast off 4 sts at beginning of next 2 rows.

Cast off 2 sts at beginning of next 2 rows.

Dec 1 st at each end of every following RS row until 20 sts remain.

Work 3 rows without shaping and leave on a spare needle.

Work front to match.

Finishing
With RS together, join crotch seam using 3-needle bind off.

Darn in all ends.

Using 2 mm crochet hook, work 1 row of double crochet around leg openings.

Sew in knitting (shirring) elastic through top of rib section if required.

Press lightly through a damp cloth.

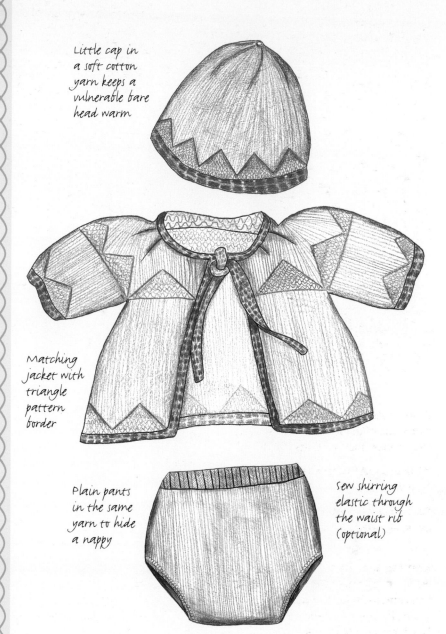

Little cap in a soft cotton yarn keeps a vulnerable bare head warm

Matching jacket with triangle pattern border

Plain pants in the same yarn to hide a nappy

sew shirring elastic through the waist rib (optional)

HINTS AND TIPS

- Fine milk cotton is perfect for this outfit, but you could substitute it with any sock yarn or even a 4-ply. For information on substituting yarn see page 138.

- For advice on knitting for premature babies, useful links and details of charities collecting donated knits, see page 134.

MATERIALS
Yarn
100 g Natural Dye Studio Dazzle sock
yarn

Needles
1 pair 3 mm needles

SIZE
To fit a 3- to 9-month-old baby

TENSION
7 sts and 11 rows over 2.5 cm (1 in)

ABBREVIATIONS
K knit
P purl
St(s) stitch(es)
Yrn yarn round needle
Tog together
Inc increase

KNITTING THE BOOTEES
Cast on 37 sts.

Starting with a k row, work 3 rows
in stocking stitch.

Shaping the Picot Edge
P1, yrn, p2tog, repeat to last st, p1.

Work in stocking stitch for 4 more rows.

Inc 1 st at beginning of next k row.

Work 9 more rows in stocking stitch.

Shaping the Instep
K25, turn.

P12.

Work these 12 sts in stocking stitch
until panel measures 4 cm (1½ ins).

Break yarn.

BOUNTIFUL BOOTEES
Stash-busting first coverings for bare feet
By Gerard Allt

I love making baby clothes. I've always knitted them for friends and family,
but this is the first time I have designed them, although I have always been
tempted by bootees. Bootees are the first thing to come to mind for babies
as it's so important that their feet are kept warm and cosy, but with the
added benefit of looking great!

These easy bootees are a brilliant way to stash-bust. Suitable for a boy or
girl, the picot edge gives a great finish to the perfect gift for a new-born.
Bootees are the perfect way to show you care about the new arrival – they
take just hours to complete.

Use any colour you like as long as you use colour – my nephews, Louis
and James, got a pair in red and white so they could show off their Liverpool
Football Club colours.

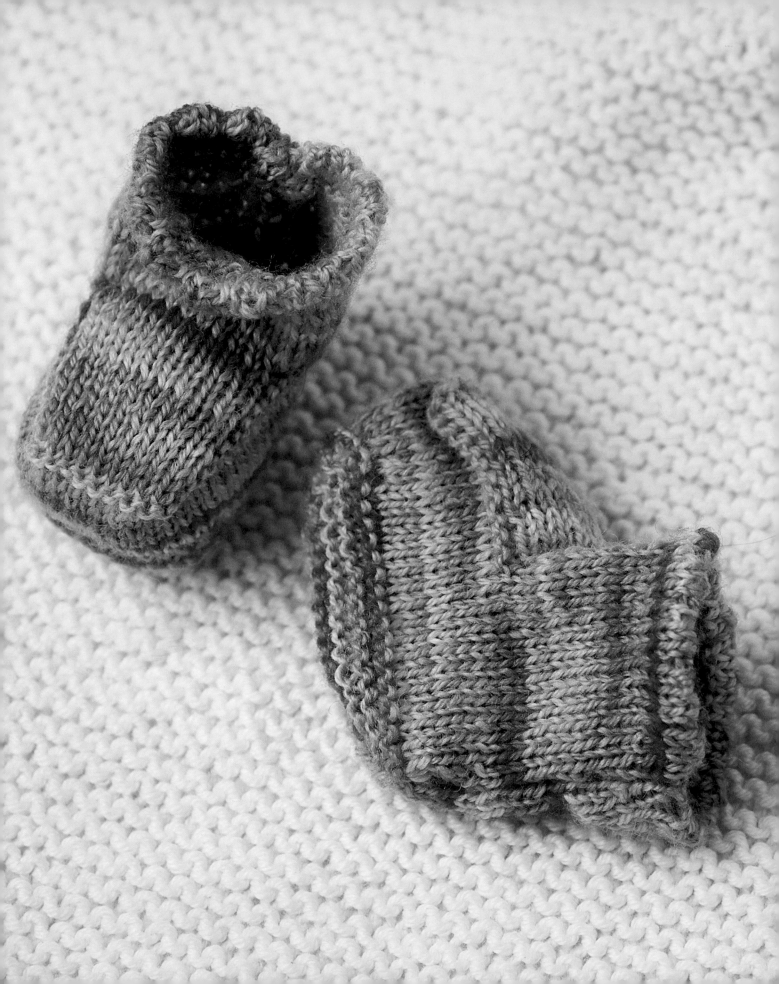

Reconnect yarn with right needle by picking up and knitting 10 sts down one side of panel, k12 sts across panel, pick up and k12 sts down other side of panel, knit to end (58 sts).

P13, k32, p13.

Starting with a k row, work 8 rows in stocking stitch.

Shaping the Sole

Sole is worked in garter stitch.

Next Row: K1, k2tog, k17, k2tog, k2tog, k10, k2tog, k2tog, k17, k2tog, k1.

Next Row: P.

Next Row: K1, k2tog, k15, k2tog, k2tog, k8, k2tog, k2tog, k15, k2tog, k1.

Next Row: P.

Next Row: K1, k2tog, k13, k2tog, k2tog, k6, k2tog, k2tog, k13, k2tog, k1.

Next Row: P.

Next Row: K1, k2tog, k11, k2tog, k2tog, k4, k2tog, k2tog, k11, k2tog, k1.

Next Row: P.

Next Row: K1, k2tog, k9, k2tog, k2tog, k2, k2tog, k2tog, k9, k2tog, k1.

Next Row: P.

Cast off.

Finishing
Sew up seam and fix cast-on edge to inside of ankle to create picot edge.

HINTS AND TIPS

- What better way to use up the oddments of your favourite sock yarns? Each bootee takes between 15 and 20 g.

- The first couple of rows after picking up the stitch on the instep will be quite tight but do not worry, it will get looser as you go. The break in the yarn can be tightened later.

- If you need a smaller bootee you could change the needle size to 2.5 mm. This needle works for most sock yarns and will give you a tighter tension and a smaller version of the bootee.

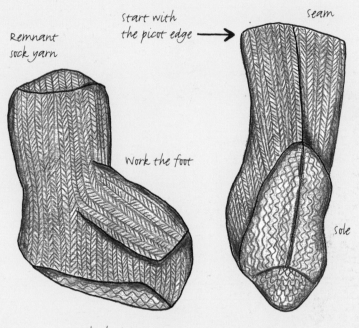

Remnant sock yarn

start with the picot edge →

seam

Work the foot

sole

Work the instep

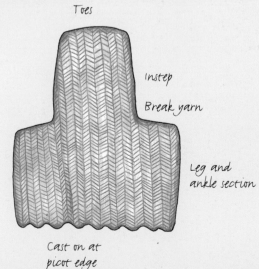

Toes

Instep

Break yarn

Leg and ankle section

Cast on at picot edge

ROSEMARY (OR ROBERT) RABBIT
An organic wool toy for a child to care for
by Judith Wright

Whether you want to show your love for a child at a time of need or just show your love anyway, this cuddly rabbit is perfect. Simply add the dress for Rosemary or omit it for Robert.

Toys are vital to a child's imagination and development. They can become someone to care for and love and represent someone else who cares for the child. Not only used for play, they can also become friends and even confidants. In psychotherapy a cherished toy is often a representation of the love between the parent and child. This toy becomes a part of the mum or dad the child can take everywhere with them and can help the child feel secure and safe in difficult situations.

Do you know a child who has to spend long periods of time in hospital, for example? They would love a cuddly toy like this.

MATERIALS

Yarn
Garthenor Organic Pure Wool:
5 x 50 g Garthenor Organic Pure Wool in Manx Lochtan (cappuccino brown) Aran (Yarn A)

2 x 50 g Garthenor Organic Pure Wool in Portland (pale cream) Aran (Yarn B)

1 x 50 g Garthenor Organic Pure Wool in Hebridean Manx (chocolate brown) Aran (Yarn C)

Needles
1 pair 4 mm needles

Other Materials
100 g organic wool toy filling

SIZE
The rabbit is 55 cm (22 ins) tall from the soles of the feet to the tips of the ears.

TENSION
8 sts and 12 rows over 4 cm (1½ ins)

ABBREVIATIONS
K knit
P purl
St(s) stitch(es)
Tog together
Beg beginning

Knitting the Rabbit

Knitting the Legs and Body (make 2)

Using Yarn A, cast on 9 sts.

* Rows 1-19: K.

Row 20: K twice into 1st st, k to last st, k twice into last st.

Repeat last 20 rows once more.

K10 rows*.

Break off yarn.

Cast on 9 sts onto same needle.

Work from * to *.

K 2 rows across both sets of sts (26 sts).

Next Row: K2 tog, k9, (k2 tog) twice, k9, k2 tog (22 sts).

K23 rows.

Next Row: K twice into 1st st, k to last st, k twice into last st.

K 2 rows.

Cast off 3 sts at beg of next 2 rows.

Cast off.

Knitting the Head (make 2)

Using Yarn A, cast on 15 sts.

K 2 rows.

Next Row: K twice into 1st st, k to end.

Next Row: K to last st, k twice into last st.

Next Row: K twice into 1st st, k to last st, k twice into last st.

K 1 row.

Repeat last 4 rows once more.

Next Row: K twice into 1st st, k to end.

Next Row: K to last st, k twice into last st.

K 8 rows.

Next Row: K2 tog, k to end.

Next Row: K to last 2 sts, k2 tog.

Repeat last 2 rows once more.

Next Row: K2 tog, k to last 2 sts, k2 tog.

Next Row: K to last 2 sts, k2 tog.

Next Row: K2 tog, k to end.

Next Row: K to last 2 sts, k2 tog.

Repeat last 4 rows once more.

Next Row: K2 tog, k to last 2 sts, k2 tog.

Cast off.

Finishing the Head

Join halves tog, leaving cast-on edge (neck edge) open.

Stuff firmly with the organic wool filling.

Gather up opening, then sew firmly to top of body.

Following the illustration on page 37, and using Yarn C, embroider features, using satin stitch for nose and running stitches for mouth and eyes.

Knitting the Ears (make 2 in Yarn A for backs and 2 in yarn B for fronts)

Cast on 3 sts.

K 1 row.

Next Row: K twice into 1st st, k to last st, k twice into last st.

K 3 rows.

Repeat last 3 rows 5 times more.

K 15 rows.

Next Row: K2 tog, k to last 2 sts, k2 tog.

K 1 row.

Next Row: K2 tog, k3, k3 tog, k3, k2 tog.

K 1 row.

Cast off.

Finishing the Ears

Join fronts to backs and sew firmly to head.

Knitting the Feet (make 2)

Using Yarn A, cast on 32 sts.

K 1 row.

Next Row: K twice into 1st st, k to last st, k twice into last st.

K 6 rows.

Next Row: K2 tog, k to last 2 sts, k2 tog.

Repeat last row twice more.

K 2 rows.

Cast off.

Finishing the Feet

Fold in half and sew tog, leaving an opening for filling.

Stuff and sew firmly to leg.

Knitting the Shoes (make 2)

Using Yarn C, work exactly as for feet.

Finishing the Shoes

Fold in half, sew together bottom seam and rounded end-seam only (leaving the top open).

Sew on a tie to each side of top cast-off edge (long enough to tie round the ankle).

(The shoes will stretch to fit over the feet.)

Knitting the Pants

Using Yarn B, cast on 50 sts.

K1 row.

Next Row: *K1, p1, repeat from * to end of row.

Repeat last row twice more.

K2 rows.

Next Row: *K4, k twice into next st, repeat from * to end of row.

K3 rows.

Next Row: *K5, k twice into next st, repeat from * to end of row.

K1 row.

Next Row: K35, turn.

** Continuing on these 35 sts, k 6 rows.

Knitting the Front Paws and Legs (make 2)

Using Yarn A, cast on 18 sts.

K 1 row.

Next Row: K twice into 1st st, k7, (k twice into next st) twice, k7, k twice into last st (22 sts).

K 6 rows.

Next Row: K2 tog, k7, (k2 tog) twice, k7, k2 tog.

K 1 row.

Next Row: K2 tog, k to last 2 sts, k2 tog.

K 20 rows.

Next Row: K twice into 1st st, k to last st, k twice into last st.

K 4 rows.

Cast off.

Finishing the Paws and Legs

Fold each piece in half lengthways and sew tog, leaving cast-off end open.

Stuff firmly and sew to body.

Following the illustration, right, and using Yarn C, embroider paws.

Next Row: K2 tog, k to end.

Next Row: *K1, p1, repeat from * to end of row.

Repeat last row once more.

Cast off.***

Rejoin yarn to remaining sts and K to end.

Work from ** to ***.

Finishing the Pants

Join leg and back seams.

Knitting the Dress Skirt

Using Yarn B, cast on 66 sts.

K 1 row.

Next Row: *K1, p1, repeat from * to end of row.

Repeat last row twice more.

Next Row: *K5, k twice into next st, repeat from * to end of row.

Next Row: *K6, k twice into next st, repeat from * to end of row.

Next Row: *K7, k twice into next st, repeat from * to end of row.

Next Row: *K8, k twice into next st, repeat from * to end of row.

K 19 rows on these 119 sts.

Cast off.

Join back seam.

Knitting the Dress Bib

Using Yarn B, cast on 19 sts.

K 20 rows.

Cast off.

Finishing the Dress

Join shoulders, leaving opening for head.

Sew cast-on edges to waist of skirt.

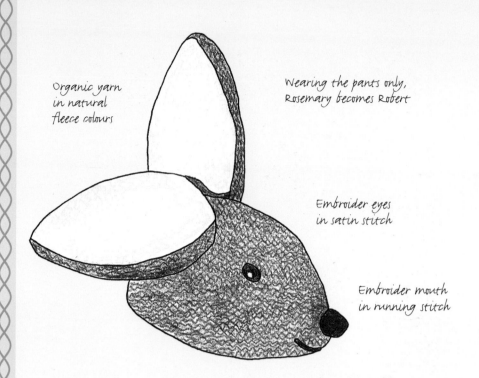

Organic yarn in natural fleece colours

Wearing the pants only, Rosemary becomes Robert

Embroider eyes in satin stitch

Embroider mouth in running stitch

HINTS AND TIPS

- The yarn used in this pattern can be substituted with any other double-knit yarn. If, for example, you would like to use a machine-washable yarn you can use Emu Superwash 100 percent wool DK.

- Teach your child to be eco-aware by telling them Rosemary's story: Rosemary is lucky enough to live in a field with her friends the Garthenor organic sheep. Everything the sheep and Rosemary eat is natural – no chemicals are used on the grass or in their food so they are all very happy and healthy. Every year, the sheep are shorn (it's a bit like getting a haircut). The shorn wool is spun into yarn in lovely colours that are the natural hues of the sheep's wool. Some of this yarn has been knitted into your very own rabbit.

Dress, pants and shoes are knitted separately

SCRATCH-FREE SWEATER
Softest alpaca cable knit for sensitive skin
by Heather Dixon

For anyone who has an allergy to the lanolin in wool, the growing availability of yarns using hypoallergenic fibres like alpaca, bamboo, soy or silk opens up the world of knits. When choosing a pattern for someone with sensitive skin, it's a good idea to look at design features as well as yarn. Heather designed a pattern without side seams and with neck ribbing that isn't too snug-fitting, to minimize rubbing. She added a striking criss-cross cable design she found in Barbara Walker's *A Fourth Treasury of Knitting Patterns,* as she loved the way the diagonals pierce the verticals. The scratch-free sweater isn't just for toddlers as Heather has supplied sizes for older children, too.

MATERIALS

Yarn
7 [7, 8, 8, 9] 50 g (100 m) skeins of Artesano 100% Alpaca DK (100% Pure Superfine Alpaca) in shade 0743

Figures in square brackets [] refer to the larger sizes. Where only one figure is given this refers to all sizes.

Needles
1 x 3.75 mm 80-cm (30 -ns) circular needle

1 x 4 mm 80-cm (30 -ns) circular needle

1 set 4 mm double-pointed needles (optional)

Tapestry needle

Stitch markers

Stitch holders

SIZE
To fit age: 2 [4, 6, 8, 10]
Actual measurement at chest: 66 [71, 76, 81, 86] cm (26 [28, 30, 32, 34] ins)

TENSION
20 sts and 29 rows over 10 cm (4 ins) over stocking stitch on 3.75 mm needles

ABBREVIATIONS
K knit
P purl
St(s) stitch(es)
Dec decrease(ing)
Inc increase(ing)

KNITTING THE SWEATER

Knitting the Body (back and front worked together in the round up to the armholes)

Using 3.75 mm needles, cast on 180 [196, 212, 224, 240] sts. Join into the round, being careful not to twist the sts, and place a stitch marker between the first and last st to mark the beginning of the round.

Rounds 1 – 8: (K2, p2) to end.

Place another stitch marker between 90th and 91st [98th and 99th , 106th and 107th , 112th and 113th , 120th and 121st] sts to mark where the other side seam would be.

Change to 4 mm needles and follow chart until work measures 20 [22, 27, 30, 33] cms (7¾ [8½, 10½, 12, 13] ins).

Chart for body (repeat whole width for front and back)

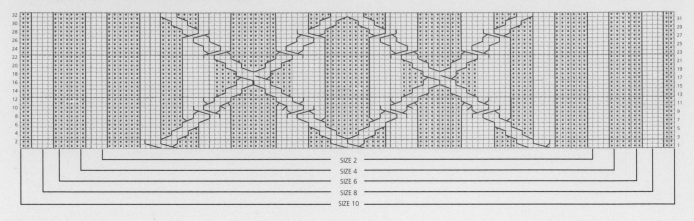

SIZE 2
SIZE 4
SIZE 6
SIZE 8
SIZE 10

Chart for Sleeve

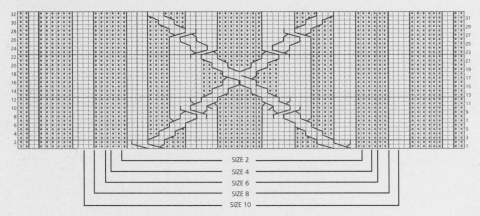

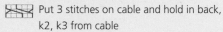
SIZE 2
SIZE 4
SIZE 6
SIZE 8
SIZE 10

KEY
- □ Knit on right side, purl on wrong side
- • Purl on right side, knit on wrong side
- Put 3 stitches on cable and hold in back, k2, k3 from cable
- Put 2 stitches on cable and hold in front, k3, k2 from cable

Shaping the Armholes

Still following chart and keeping pattern correct, work on upper back sts in rows before returning to work on sts for upper front.

Next Row: Cast off 5 [5, 5, 5, 6] sts, work to marker, remove marker, turn, leaving sts for front on a holder, cast off 5 [5, 5, 5, 6] sts, work to marker, remove marker.

Cast off 4 sts at beginning of next 2 rows.

Dec 1 st at each end of next and following alternate rows 1 [1, 1, 2, 2] times (68 [76, 84, 88, 94] sts).

Continue on these sts until work measures 14 [17, 18, 19, 20] cm (5½ [6¾, 7¼, 7½, 8] ins) from armhole shaping, ending with a wrong side row.

Shaping the Shoulders

Still following chart and keeping pattern correct, cast off 6 [7, 7, 8, 9] sts at beginning of next 2 rows.

Cast off 5 [6, 7, 8, 8] sts at beginning of next 2 rows.

Cast off 5 [6, 6, 7, 8] sts at beginning of next 2 rows.

Cast off remaining 36 [38, 44, 42, 44] sts.

Return to 90 [98, 106, 112, 120] sts on holder.

Cast off 5 [5, 5, 5, 6] sts at beginning of next 2 rows.

Cast off 4 sts at beginning of next 2 rows.

Dec 1 st at each end of next and following alternate rows 1 [1, 1, 2, 2] times (68 [76, 84, 88, 94] sts).

Continue on these sts until work measures 10 [13, 14.5, 15, 16.5] cm (4 [5¼, 5¾, 6, 6½] ins) from armhole shaping, ending with a wrong side row.

Dividing for the Neck

Still following chart and keeping pattern correct, work across 27 [28, 30, 32, 35] sts, cast off 14 [20, 24, 24, 24] sts for neck then work to end of row.

Work on each side of neck separately.

Work 1 row.

Cast off 3 sts at beg of next and following 1 [0, 0, 0, 0] alternate rows.

Work 1 row.

Cast off 2 sts at beginning of next and following 0 [1, 1, 1, 1] alternate rows.

Dec 1 st at neck edge on next and following 2 [1, 2, 1, 2] rows (16 [19, 20, 23, 25] sts).

Continue on these sts until work measures same as back to start of shoulder shaping, ending with a RS row for start of shoulder shaping.

Shaping the Shoulders

Still following chart and keeping pattern correct, cast off 6 [7, 7, 8, 9] sts at beginning of next row.

Work 1 row.

Cast off 5 [6, 7, 8, 8] sts at beginning of next row.

Work 1 row.

Cast off remaining sts.

Rejoin yarn at left side of neck and work shaping to match right side.

Knitting the Sleeves

(worked in the round up to the armholes)
Using 3.75 mm needles, cast on 42 [46, 48, 52, 56] sts.

Join into a round, being careful not to twist the sts and place a stitch marker between the first and last st to mark the beginning of the round.

For sizes 2, 4 and 6 only:

Rounds 1 – 8: K2, (p2, k2) to end.

Sizes 8 and 10 only:

Rounds 1–8: (K2, p2) to end.

All sizes:

Change to 4 mm needles and follow chart, inc 1 st at beginning and end of rounds as marked, then continue without shaping until work measures 30.5 [33, 35.5, 38, 40.5] cm (12 [13, 14, 15, 16] ins), ending with an even-numbered round.

Shaping the Armhole

From now on you will be working back and forth in rows.

Cast off 5 [5, 5, 5, 6] sts at beginning of next 2 rows.

Cast off 4 sts at beginning of next 2 rows.

Dec 1 st at each end of next and following 1 [1, 1, 2, 2] alternate rows (58 [68, 72, 74, 80] sts.

Sizes 6, 8 and 10 only:

Work 1 row.

Dec 1 st at each end of every 4th row 0 [0, 2, 2, 3] times.

All sizes:

Work 1 row.

Dec 1 st at each end of next and following alternate row 1 [4, 3, 4, 3] times.

Work 1 row.

Cast off 2 sts at beginning of next 4 [2, 4, 4, 4] rows.

Cast off 3 sts at beginning of next 2 [2, 2, 2, 4] rows.

Cast off 4 sts at beginning of next 6 rows.

Cast off remaining 16 [24, 22, 22, 22] sts.

Sew shoulder seams.

Sew in sleeves.

Shaping the Neck

Using 3.75 mm needles, with RS facing and starting at left shoulder seam, pick up and k12 [12, 12, 13, 14] sts down left front, 14 [20, 24, 24, 24] sts across centre front, 12 [12, 12, 13, 14] sts up right front and 36 [38, 44, 42, 44] sts of back (74 [82, 92, 92, 96] sts).

Join into a round, placing marker between first and last sts.

Rounds 1 – 5: (K1, p1) to end.

Cast off neatly in pattern.

Finishing

Sew in all loose ends neatly.
Block to shape if necessary.

HINTS AND TIPS

- For information on other yarns suitable for those allergic to wool, dyes or processes and a listing of projects in this book using allergy-free yarns see page 134.

- Don't be afraid to use stitch markers; once you get used to them they make counting and following complicated patterns much easier. They go on the needle, between the stitches, and when you get to them you just move them from one needle to the other and then keep knitting. You can simply use a length of coloured yarn, buy inexpensive plain plastic discs, or indulge in the hand-crafted decorative sort.

Angel hand-crafted stitch marker

Bead stitch markers

Treats for Kids & Teens

HAPPY HAT
Fast and easy cap for a child to knit

by Judith More

A chunky hat is easy, stylish and fun. It's a great way to introduce a child to the art of knitting, too. Especially if you use a fabulous chunky yarn! This consists of a rectangle with a simple rib and stocking stitch design topped with a trio of pom-poms swinging from a yarn plait.

The hat is knitted flat, making it the perfect first project. Feel free to add as many pom-poms as you wish. Children love pom-poms, and making the project as positive and entertaining as possible will mean they keep on knitting.

MATERIALS

Yarn
100 g Rowan Big Wool in Bohemian 028 (red)

Oddments of Rowan Little Big Wool in contrasting colours

Needles
1 x 10 mm circular needle
Yarn finishing needle

Other Materials
Pom-pom maker or cardboard

SIZE
To fit an 8-12 year ond child, or a teen

TENSION
5 sts and 7 rows over 5 cm (2 ins)

ABBREVIATIONS
K knit
P purl
St(s) stitch(es)

KNITTING THE HAT
Cast on 60 sts.

Work 6 rows in k1, p1 rib.

Work 20 rows in stocking stitch.

Cast off.

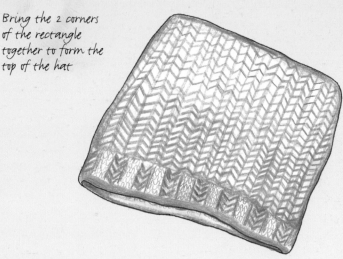

Bring the 2 corners of the rectangle together to form the top of the hat

HINTS AND TIPS

- If your child finds the 10 mm needles just a little bit too big, there are many chunky yarns that you may use with smaller needles – just increase the number of cast-on stitches.

Making the Pom-Pom Tail

To make the balls, if you are using a pom-pom maker, follow the manufacturer's instructions. For a home-made cardboard version see the illustrations right.

Make 3 balls in the same way.

Plait together the tails left by the yarn ties.

Finishing

Working on the wrong side, sew side and top seam, leaving a small gap on one corner of the top seam for the plait of pom-poms. Thread through and sew in place.

Thread the plait through to the wrong side, leaving the main length and the pom-poms on the right side, and secure the free end of the plait with a few stitches.

Turn right side out and stitch together the two corners to form the top of the hat.

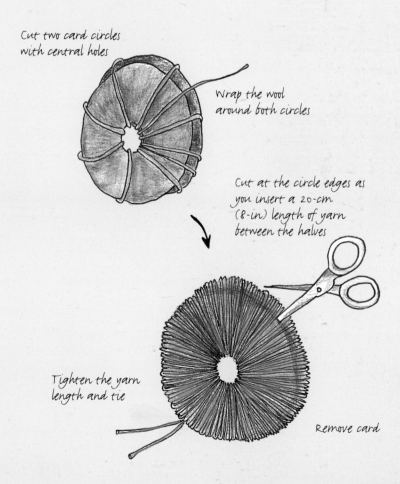

Cut two card circles with central holes

Wrap the wool around both circles

Cut at the circle edges as you insert a 20-cm (8-in) length of yarn between the halves

Tighten the yarn length and tie

Remove card

RED-HOT CHILLI SCARF
Fun-shaped scarf to warm a travelling teen
by Gerard Allt

Scarves are usually the first thing that we make as a new knitter. They can be a great way to practise and get used to the needles and the yarn. A scarf is an easy item – cast on and knit until you run out of yarn, or until you run out of steam! You can make one quickly for a perfect last-minute gift, too.

Not all scarves have to be mindless knitting, though. This cool scarf will raise the temperature of any child with the fun element, the bright colours and the softness of the alpaca. The shaping of the scarf will keep you entertained until the last stitch!

The scarf is knitted with a 4-stitch stocking stitch border and moss stitch body. The scarf can be any length or width you prefer.

MATERIALS

Yarn
100 g double-knit alpaca in Red (Yarn A)

Small amount of double knit alpaca in Green (Yarn B)

Needles
1 pair 4 mm needles

TENSION
7 sts and 8 rows over 4 cm (1½ ins)

ABBREVIATIONS
K knit
P purl
St(s) stitch(es)
M make (increase)
M1P make 1 purlwise
M1K make 1 knitwise
K2tog knit 2 together

KNITTING THE SCARF
Using Yarn A, cast on 3 sts.

Work 2 rows in stocking stitch.

Shaping the Tail
Row 3: K1, m1, k1, m1, k1.
Row 4: P.
Row 5: K2, m1, k1, m1, k2.
Row 6: P.
Row 7: K3, m1, p1, m1, k3.
Row 8: P4, k1, p4.
Row 9: K4, m1p, k5.
Row 10: P4, k1, p5.
Row 11: K4, m1k, p1, k5.
Row 12: P4, k1, p1, k1, p4.
Row 13: K4, m1p, m1, p1, k5.
Row 14: P4, k1, p1, k1, p5.
Row 15: K4, m1k, p1, k1, p1, k5.
Row 16: P4, k1, p1, k1, p1, k1, p4.
Row 17: K4, m1p, k1, p1, k1, p1, k5.
Row 18: P4, k1, p1, k1, p1, k1, p5.
Row 19: K4, m1k, p1, k1, p1, k1, p1, k5.

Continue to increase after 4-st border on rows beginning K and staying in pattern as set for centre panel with 4-st end border until you have 35 sts, or desired length.

Shaping the Centre Panel

Continuing in pattern as set, introduce a decrease at the end of every increase row as follows:

1st Row: K4, m1, moss stitch to last 6 st, k2tog, k4.

2nd Row: P4, moss stitch to last 4 sts, p4.

Repeat these 2 rows 35 times or to desired length.

Increase at both ends of next and every alternate 4th row 10 times, or to desired length.

Shaping the Top

1st Row: K1, k2tog 4 times, k to last 9 stitches, k2tog 4 times, k1.

2nd Row: P.

Repeat these 2 rows 3 times more.

Adding the Green Stem

The green stem is worked on the centre sts of the end of the chilli. The stem should be no less than 25 sts, so find the centre 25 sts (or more depending on size and length of finished scarf).

Still using Yarn A, cast off the number of stitches needed to reach the centre 25-st panel for stem.

Break off yarn.

Using Yarn B, k the required number of stitches for the beginning of your stem (at least 25).

Using Yarn A, cast off the rest of the stitches on the row (the number should be the same on either side of stem).

Pick up Yarn B and P.

Next Row: K1, k2 tog twice, k to last 5 sts, k2tog twice, k1.

Next Row: P.

Repeat these 2 rows twice more.

Next Row: K1, k2tog, k to last 3 sts, k2tog, k1.

Cast off.

- This yarn can be substituted with any double knit, but if you want to use a favourite yarn that is a different weight you can simply adjust the number of increases you put in the scarf.

- Making sure that the moss stitch pattern remains when increasing can be a little tricky for less experienced knitters, so take a little extra care by checking each row as you work the scarf until you get used to the patterning.

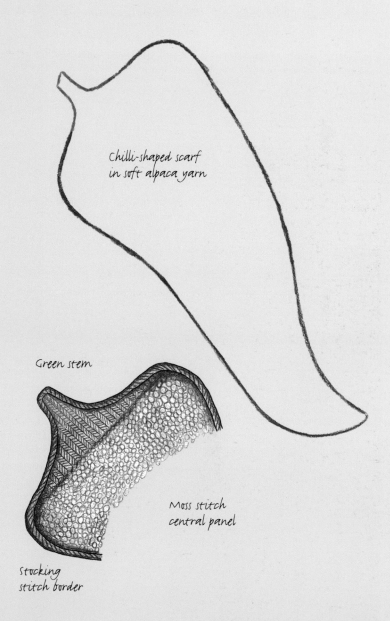

Chilli-shaped scarf in soft alpaca yarn

Green stem

Moss stitch central panel

stocking stitch border

GOOD HABITS HANDBAG
Bucket bag made from recycled carriers
by Emily Blades

Recycling, reusing and reclaiming are activities that more and more of us are adopting out of concern over the shockingly large mountain of plastic piling up in landfill sites. Knitting with plastic reclaimed from store carriers is just as rewarding as knitting with yarn and has the additional benefit of reducing waste.

This bag is a brilliant gift for any young woman with a sense of style and a concern for the environment. By the nature of the yarn, each bag will be absolutely unique and personal to whom ever you present it to – choose colours that suit their wardrobe and personality.

MATERIALS

Plastic carrier bags and metallic food bags cut into strips 2 cm (³/₄ in) wide
Stiff cardboard

Needles
1 x 4 mm circular knitting needle
1 x 4 mm crochet hook

SIZE

Height: 42 cm (16½ ins)
Width: 38 cm (15 ins)

TENSION

No need to measure your tension for this one: just knit a swatch to make sure that your knitting produces a firm fabric, with no holes for things to slip through. If it is too loose, switch to smaller needles until the result is tight enough. If you prefer looser tension, line the bag.

KNITTING THE BAG

In single crochet stitch, make 2 circular mats, each the size wanted for the base of the handbag, e.g.14 cm (5½ ins) in diameter.

Cut out a circular piece of cardboard slightly smaller than the mats.

Sandwich the cardboard between the mats and stitch together around the edge, enclosing the card. This will give a firm crochet-covered base.

With a circular needle, pick up and knit stitches all around the base.

Working in stocking stitch (i.e. knit every round), continue until the desired depth is reached.

Cast off.

Finishing
Sew on fancy handles with strips of matching plastic.

HINTS AND TIPS

- For instructions on how to make plastic 'yarn' see page 139.

- Some supermarkets now provide biodegradable bags, which disintegrate after a few months. Avoid using these, so that all your hard work doesn't just disappear.

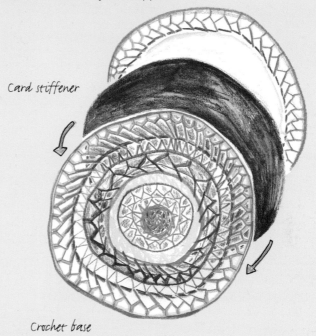

Card stiffener

Crochet base

Fancy handles

Knit main part of bag in stocking stitch

FLOWER FASCINATOR

A pretty posy to celebrate a milestone

By Susan Ryder

I love this fascinator! I have a hope that one day I will take my mum and dad and my god-daughter, Iris, to Liverpool's Aintree for a day at the races. Of course my sisters would have to come, too! It would be The Grand National, obviously, and it would be a surprise. (Maybe less of a surprise now!) My dad likes a little flutter and I think my mum would love the excitement and the glamour of the VIP grandstand enclosure overlooking the famous water jump.

Naturally, the added extra to this day out would be the fascinator made by my own fair hand. Iris, a true princess, would be the belle of the ball wearing this.

Yarn
1 ball Rowan Kidsilk Haze in pink (Yarn A)

1 ball Rowan Kidsilk Haze in green (Yarn B)

Needles
1 pair 4 mm needles

Crochet hooks
1 x 3 mm crochet hook
1 x 5 mm crochet hook

Other materials
1 piece of Merry Widow veiling
1 piece of felt
Matching thread
1 hair clip

Note: Instructions for a crochet version are included alongside the knitting pattern for this design.

ABBREVIATIONS
Tr treble crochet
Dc double crochet
St(s) stitch(es)
Sl slip
Dec decrease
Incr increase
YO yarn over

MAKING A KNITTED FASCINATOR

Large flower (make 1)
Cast on 136 sts using Yarn A.

1st Row: K.

2nd Row: *K3, K1, slip this st back onto left-hand needle, then lift 8 sts individually over knitted st, YO twice, repeat * to end of row.

3rd row: *K1, p2tog, drop 1 YO off needle, **k into front of 2nd YO stitch, leave on needle, P1 into st, ** repeat once, drop YO off st. From * repeat to end of row.

4th-11th row: K.

Cast off.

Small flower (make 2)
Cast on 68 sts using Yarn A.

1st and 2nd rows: work row 2 and 3 of large flower.

Rows 3-6: K.
Cast off.

Leaf (make 6)
Cast on 2 sts using Yarn B.

1st Row: K.

2nd Row: *Inc 1, K1*; repeat from * to * to end of row.

3rd Row: K

4th Row: *Inc 1, K1*; repeat from * to * to end of row.

5th Row: K.

6th Row: *Inc 1, K1*; repeat from * to * to end of row (8 sts.)

Rows 7-12: K.

13th Row: *Dec 1, K1*; repeat from * to *. to end of row.

14th Row: K.

15th Row: *Dec 1, K1*; repeat from * to * to end of row.

16th Row: K.

17th Row: *Dec 1, K1*; repeat from * to * to end of row.

18th Row: K.

Cast off.

MAKING A CROCHET FASCINATOR

Large Flower (make 1)
Using 5 mm hook and Yarn A, chain 41.

Row 1: Tr into 4th chain from hook, *2tr in next chain, repeat from * to end of row.

Row 2: Chain 2, * 1dc in 1st st, 1tr into next st, 1dc into next st, 1tr into next st, repeat from * to end.

Row 3: Chain 6, sl st into 4th st, *chain 6, miss 3 sts, then sl st into 4th st, repeat from * to end.

Row 4: Sl st around the chain, 3dc around the chain, 3tr around the chain, 3dc around the chain, sl st around the chain. Repeat this around every chain and fasten off.

Small flower (make 2)
Using 3 mm hook and Yarn B, follow instructions for large flower.

Leaf (make 6)
Using 3 mm hook and Yarn B, chain 4.

Row 1: 2tr into 1st chain furthest from the hook.

Row 2: Chain 3, 2tr into each stitch.

Row 3: Chain 3, 2tr into 1st st, 1tr into all but last st, 2tr.

Repeat Row 4 three times.

Row 7: 1tr into each stitch until halfway along the row, dec, then 1tr to the end of the row. Don't worry if you are not in the exact centre of the row, as any variation adds to the organic look of the shape.

Repeat Row 7 until there is 1 st left on hook. Fasten off.

Finishing for both versions
See page 59.

HINTS AND TIPS

- This item is all about the yarn. For extra sparkle you could use a fancy yarn that incorporates metallic thread or beads, such as Kidsilk Night or Kraemer Silk and Silver (with real sterling silver!) or maybe even Tilli Tomas beaded lace, for luxury and elegance.

- The lovely thing about this pattern is that you can easily modify it, not just by changing the colour but by altering the size or the number of flowers you use, or even the purpose. Why not use a brooch back instead of a hair clip? Or the flowers could be put together into a buttonhole for a man to wear in his suit – just the thing for a stylish family going for a day at the races! Besides, I don't like being left out!

Finishing

Sew in loose ends. Roll up each strip (see right). Sew the leaves to the base of each flower.

Cut felt small enough to be concealed beneath the flowers but large enough to attach the flowers and clip.

Cut a square of net, pinch in the middle, and sew around the pinched section. Sew the net to the felt, sewing roughly in the middle.

Sew the flowers over the net, through the felt. Depending on clip type, glue or sew the felt onto the back of the clip.

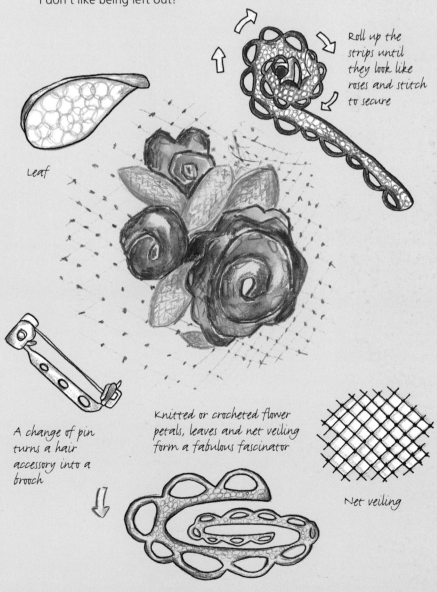

Roll up the strips until they look like roses and stitch to secure

Leaf

A change of pin turns a hair accessory into a brooch

Knitted or crocheted flower petals, leaves and net veiling form a fabulous fascinator

Net veiling

For Women to Treasure

A SHAWL FULL OF GOOD WISHES

Triangular wrap stitched with love

by Sue Hawkins

Lace knitting is enjoying a renaissance, with many knitters discovering the rewards and finding out that it doesn't always have to be as complicated as it looks! Investing the time in knitting a shawl for someone you cherish is only part of the gift. There's a sense of immediate security when wrapped in a favourite shawl, and this, coupled with the luxurious laceweight silky yarn, is an unbeatable combination.

Using intricate motifs and lace patterns, your shawl can symbolize character, personality and relationship. The motifs can reinforce a positivity that is often difficult to express by giving any other gift. The leaf motif employed here is symbolic of nature; life-giving, nurturing and a source of energy. This shawl is the perfect gift for your guardian angel.

MATERIALS

Yarn
1 skein of Knitwitches
Seriously Gorgeous Laceweight
2-ply Silk 100 g/600 m

Needles
1 x 3.5 mm circular needle

TENSION
There is no need to knit a swatch as
tension is not important with this design

SIZE
Approximately 106 cm X 106 cm X 132
cm (42 ins x 42 ins x 52 ins)

ABBREVIATIONS
K knit
P purl
YO yarn over needle

KNITTING THE SHAWL

Cast on 4 sts.

Working the Pattern

1st Row: K2, yo, k2.

2nd Row: K2, p1, k2.

3rd Row: K2, yo, k1, yo, k2.

4th Row: K2, p3, k2.

5th Row: K2, yo, k3, yo, k2.

6th Row: K2, p5, k2.

Left hand side of shawl

Repeat as required

Right hand side of shawl

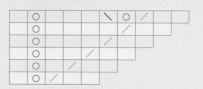

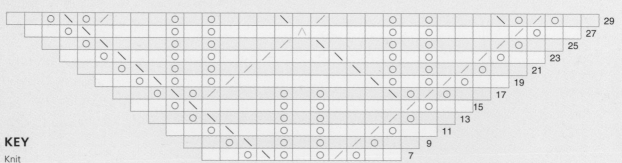

29
27
25
23
21
19
17
15
13
11
9
7

KEY

⬜ Knit

◯ yarn over

╱ Knit two together

╲ slip 1, knit 1, pass slip stitch over

∧ slip 1, knit 2 tog, pass slip stitch over

* The shawl will benefit from blocking – pin it out to an even shape on ironing felt or a towel, place a damp cloth over it and then gently press with a hot iron.

* The lace bind-off described in the method, left, can be used for non-lace projects too. Why not try it for socks if you have a tendency to cast off too tightly as it creates a looseish edge.

7th Row: Start working from chart, noting only right-side rows are shown.

Note: The first two and last two stitches of every row are knitted.

On all wrong side rows knit 2, purl to last two stitches, knit 2.

There is an extra increase (yarn over) when a new leaf is started (beginning and end of the row).

Continue repeating six rows of chart (12 rows of work), incorporating extra stitches into further repeats.

Work 4 rows of plain knit, then cast off using a lace cast-off:

K2, * pass sts back to left needle, k2tog, K1

Repeat across row, finishing off last st.

Finishing
Block shawl and enjoy.

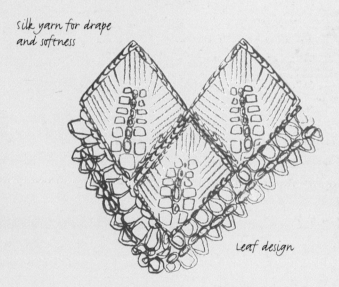

silk yarn for drape and softness

Leaf design

MATERIALS

Yarn

11 [12,12,13,13] 50 g (105m) skeins of Knit One Crochet Too Babyboo in shade 570 Lime

Other Materials

26 buttons

Needles

1 x 3.75 mm 120-cm (48-in) circular needle

I set 3.75 mm double-pointed needles

Tapestry needle
Stitch markers
Stitch holders

SIZE

To fit bust: 81–86 [91–97, 102–107, 112–122, 127–132] cm (32–34 [36–38, 40–42, 44–48, 50–52] ins).

Actual width at bust: 40.5 [46, 51, 56, 63.5] cm (16 [18, 20, 22, 25] ins)

Length: 63.5 [66, 69, 71, 74] cm (25 [26, 27, 28, 29] ins)

Figures in square brackets [] refer to the larger sizes. Where only one figure is given, this refers to all sizes.

TENSION

22 sts and 29 rows over 10 cm (4 ins) over stocking stitch

ABBREVIATIONS

K knit
P purl
St(s) stitch(es)
PM place marker
RM remove marker
Inc increase(ing)
Dec decrease(ing)
M1 make 1 stitch
SM slip marker
YF yarn forward
SSK slip, slip, knit (slip 2 stitches, insert left needle into front of slipped stitches, knit together through the back loops)
KFB knit in front and back of stitch
Rep Repeat

TO MATERNITY & BEYOND
A sweater that expands through pregnancy
by Heather Dixon

If you have a friend who is wondering what to wear as the baby bulge is steadily growing, then why not knit her this sweater she can wear through maternity and beyond. The soft bamboo-mix yarn is cooler to wear than a wool yarn – pregnant women often feel hot – and easy to wash. The convertible design means that she can button in the side panels as she grows then take them out again when the bump is gone. The plunging neckline makes the most of the heaving cleavage that accompanies the belly!

KNITTING THE SWEATER

Knitting the Body

Cast on 36 [46, 56, 66, 76] sts.

Row 1: (K1, p1) to last 2 sts, k2.

Row 2: K1 (k1, p1) to last st, k1.

Rep Rows 1 and 2 twice, then Row 1 once more.

Row 8 (inc): K1, pm, k1, pm, m1, k6 [8, 10, 12, 14], m1, pm, k1, pm, m1, k4 [7, 10, 13, 16], pm (k1, p1) 5 times, pm, k4 [7, 10, 13, 16], m1, pm, k1, pm, m1, k6 [8, 10, 12, 14], m1, pm, k1, pm, k1 (42 [52, 62, 72, 82] sts).

Row 9: K1, p to 5th marker (p1, k1) 5 times, p to last st, k1.

Row 10 (inc): K1, m1, k1, m1, k to 3rd marker, m1, k1, m1, k to 5th marker (k1, p1) 5 times, k to 7th marker, m1, k1, m1, k to 9th marker, m1, k1, m1, k1 (50 [60, 70, 80, 90] sts).

Row 11: K2, p to 5th marker (p1, k1) 5 times, p to last 2 sts, k2.

Row 12 (inc):): K to 2nd marker, sm, m1, k to 3rd marker, m1, k1, m1, k to 5th marker (k1, p1) 5 times, k to 7th marker, m1, k1, m1, k to 9th marker, m1, k to end (56 [66, 76, 86, 96] sts).

Row 13: K2, p to 5th marker (p1, k1) 5 times, p to last 2 sts, k2.

Rep rows 12 and 13 six more times (92 [102, 112, 122, 132] sts).

Row 26 (inc): K to 1st marker, m1, k1, m1, k to 3rd marker, m1, k1, m1, k to 5th marker (k1, p1) 5 times, k to 7th marker, m1, k1, m1, k to 9th marker, m1, k1, m1, k to end (100 [110, 120, 130, 140] sts).

Row 27: As Row 13.

Row 28 (inc): K2, p1, k1, sm, m1, k to 5th marker (k1, p1) 5 times, k to 7th marker, m1, k1, m1, k to 9th marker, m1, k1, p1, k2 (106 [116, 126, 136, 146] sts).

Row 29: As Row 13.

Row 30 (inc): K2, p1, m1, k1, m1, k to 3rd marker, m1, k1, m1, k to 5th marker (k1, p1) 5 times, k to 7th marker, m1, k1, m1, k to 9th marker, m1, k1, m1, p1, k2 (114 [124, 134, 144, 154] sts).

Row 31: K2, p1, k1, p to 5th marker (p1, k1) 5 times, p to last 4 sts, k1, p1, k2.

Row 32 (inc): K2, p1, k1, m1, k1, m1, k to 3rd marker, m1, k1, m1, k to 5th marker (k1, p1) 5 times, k to 7th marker, m1, k1, m1, k to 9th marker, m1, k1, m1, k1, p1, k2 (122 [132, 142, 152, 162] sts).

Row 33: K1 (k1, p1) twice, p to 5th marker (p1, k1) 5 times, p to last 5 sts (p1, k1), twice, k1.

Row 34 (inc): K1, m1 (k1, p1) twice, m1, k1, m1, k to 3rd marker, m1, k1, m1, k to 5th marker (k1, p1) 5 times, k to 7th marker, m1, k1, m1, k to 9th marker, m1, k1, m1 (p1, k1) twice, m1, k1 (132 [142, 152, 162, 172] sts).

Row 35: (K1, p1) 3 times, k1, p to 5th marker (p1, k1) 5 times, p to last 7 sts (k1, p1) 3 times, k1.

Row 36 (inc): K1, m1 (p1, k1) 3 times, m1, k1, m1, k to 3rd marker, m1, k1, m1, k to 5th marker (k1, p1) 5 times, k to 7th marker, m1, k1, m1, k to 9th marker, m1, k1, m1 (k1, p1) 3 times, m1, k1 (142 [152, 162, 172, 182] sts).

Row 37: K1 (k1, p1) 4 times, p to 5th marker (p1, k1) 5 times, p to last 9 sts (p1, k1) 4 times, k1.

Row 38 (inc): K1, m1 (k1, p1) 4 times, m1, k1, m1, k to 3rd marker, m1, k1, m1, k to 5th marker (k1, p1) 5 times, k to 7th marker, m1, k1, m1, k to 9th marker, m1, k1, m1 (p1, k1) 4 times, m1, k1 (152 [162, 172, 182, 192] sts).

Row 39: (K1, p1) 5 times, k1, p to 5th marker (p1, k1) 5 times, p to last 11 sts (k1, p1) 5 times, k1.

Row 40 (inc): K1, m1 (p1, k1) 5 times, m1, k1, m1, k to 3rd marker, m1, k1, m1, k to 5th marker, (k1, p1) 5 times, k to 7th marker, m1, k1, m1, k to 9th marker, m1,

k1, m1, (k1, p1) 5 times, m1, k1 (162 [172, 182, 192, 202] sts).

Row 41: K1 (k1, p1) 6 times, p to 5th marker (p1, k1) 5 times, p to last 13 sts (p1, k1) 6 times, k1.

Row 42 (inc): K1, m1 (k1, p1) 6 times, m1, k1, m1, k to 3rd marker, m1, k1, m1, k to 5th marker (k1, p1) 5 times, k to 7th marker, m1, k1, m1, k to 9th marker, m1, k1, m1 (p1, k1) 6 times, m1, k1 (172 [182, 192, 202, 212] sts).

Row 43: (K1, p1) 7 times, k1, p to 5th marker (p1, k1) 5 times, p to last 15 sts (k1, p1) 7 times, k1.

Row 44 (inc): K1, m1 (p1, k1) 7 times, m1, k1, m1, k to 3rd marker, m1, k1, m1, k to 5th marker (k1, p1) 5 times, k to 7th marker, m1, k1, m1, k to 9th marker, m1, k1, m1 (k1, p1) 7 times, m1, k1 (182 [192, 202, 212, 222] sts).

Row 45: K1 (k1, p1) 8 times, p to 5th marker (p1, k1) 5 times, p to last 17 sts (p1, k1) 8 times, k1.

Row 46 (inc): K1, m1 (k1, p1) 8 times, m1, k1, m1, k to 3rd marker, m1, k1, m1, k to 5th marker (k1, p1) 5 times, k to 7th marker, m1, k1, m1, k to 9th marker, m1, k1, m1 (p1, k1) 8 times, m1, k1 (192 [202, 212, 222, 232] sts).

Row 47: (K1, p1) 9 times, k1, p to 5th marker (p1, k1) 5 times, p to last 19 sts (k1, p1) 9 times, k1.

Row 48 (inc): K1, m1 (p1, k1) 9 times, m1, k1, m1, k to 3rd marker, m1, k1, m1, k to 5th marker (k1, p1) 5 times, k to 7th marker, m1, k1, m1, k to 9th marker, m1, k1, m1 (k1, p1) 9 times, m1, k1 (202 [212, 222, 232, 242] sts).

Row 49: K1 (k1, p1) 10 times, p to 5th marker (p1, k1) 5 times, p to last 21 sts (p1, k1) 10 times, k1.

Continue to work as set, inc 10 sts on each RS row until sts before first marker equal half the amount of sts between 4th and 7th markers, ending with a RS row (292 [332, 372, 412, 452] sts).

Joining the Fronts

Keeping moss st pattern correct, join work into a round by working across sts for upper left front directly after end of last row, work in moss st to next marker, m, k1, rm, turn. Cast on 5 sts, turn.

Row 2: K1, then keeping moss st correct, work across all front sts to next marker, rm, p1, cast on 5 sts, turn, leaving all sts for sleeves and back on a holder.

Keeping moss st correct, **and** knitting first and last sts, work on front section for another 2 rows.

Row 5 (buttonhole row): K1, p1, yf, k2tog, continue working in moss st to last 3 sts, yf, k2tog, k1.

Work 19 rows in moss st.

Row 25 (inc and buttonhole row): K1, p1, yf, k2tog, p1, k35 [41, 48, 53, 59] (m1, k1) 10 times, k to last 5sts, p1, k2tog, yf, k2 (100 [112, 124, 136, 148] sts).

Row 26: K1 (k1, p1) twice, p to last 5 sts (p1, k1) twice, k1.

Row 27: K1 (k1, p1) twice, k to last 5 sts (p1, k1) twice, k1.

Rep Rows 26 and 27 eight times, then Row 26 once.

Row 45 (buttonhole row): K1, p1, yf, k2tog, p1, k to last 5 sts, p1, k2tog, yf, k2.

Rep last 18 rows 4 times. Rep Rows 26 and 27 twice, then Row 26 once.

Row 123: K1 (k1, p1) to last st, k1.

Row 124: (K1, p1) to last 2 sts, k2.

Rep last 2 rows twice more.
Cast off in pattern.

Knitting the Back

Return to centre 80 [92 104 116 128] held sts (keeping sts for both sleeves on holder, removing all markers as you get to them).

With RS facing, cast on 5 sts, k1 (k1, p1) twice, k to 10 centre moss sts (p1, k1) 5 times, k to end, turn.

Cast on 5 sts (k1, p1) twice, k1, p to 10 centre moss sts (k1, p1) 5 times, p to last 5 sts (p1, k1) twice, k1 (90 [102, 114, 126, 138] sts).

Row 3: K1 (k1, p1) twice, k to 10 centre moss sts (p1, k1) 5 times, k to last 5 sts (k1, p1) twice, k1.

Row 4: (K1, p1) twice, k1, p to 10 centre moss sts (k1, p1) 5 times, p to last 5 sts (p1, k1) twice, k1.

Rep Rows 3 and 4 seven times.

Row 19: K1 (k1, p1) twice, k to 10 centre moss sts, k2 (p1, k1) 3 times, k to last 5 sts (k1, p1) twice, k1.

Row 20: ((K1, p1) twice, k1, p to 6 centre moss sts (k1, p1) 3 times, p to last 5 sts (p1, k1) twice, k1.

Row 21: K1 (k1, p1) twice, k to 6 centre moss sts k2, p1, k to last 5 sts (k1, p1) twice, k1.

Row 22: (K1, p1) twice, k1, p to 2 centre moss sts k1, p to last 5 sts (p1, k1) twice, k1.

Row 23: : K1 (k1, p1) twice, k to last 5 sts (k1, p1) twice, k1.

Row 24: (K1, p1) twice, k1, p to last 5 sts (p1, k1) twice, k1.

Rep Rows 23 and 24 forty-nine times.

Row 123: K1 (k1, p1) to last st, k1.

Row 124: (K1, p1) to last 2 sts, k2.

Rep last 2 rows twice more.
Cast off in pattern.

Knitting the Sleeves

Right sleeve only

With RS facing, k across sts for right sleeve (leaving sts for left sleeve on holder), then pick up and k 5 sts from top of moss st buttonhole band of side front.

** PM, join into a round and k 7 rounds.

Round 9 (dec). Ssk, k to 2 sts from end, k2tog.
K 6 rounds.
Rep last 7 rounds 11 times.
Work without shaping until sleeve measures 42 [43, 44, 45, 46] cm (16½ [17, 17½, 17¾ , 18] ins) from underarm.

Next Round: (K1, p1) to end.

Next Round: (P1, k1) to end.

Rep last 2 rows 5 more times.
Cast off in pattern.

Left sleeve only

With RS facing, pick up and k 5 sts from top of moss st buttonhole band of side front, then k across sts for left sleeve.

Work as for Right Sleeve from **.

Knitting the Side Panels (make 2)

Cast on 5 sts.

Rows 1 – 3: (K1, p1) twice, k1.

Row 4 (buttonhole row): K1, p1, yf, k2tog, k1.

Row 5: K2, p2, k1.

Row 6 (inc): K1, p1, kfb, k2 (6 sts).

Row 7: K1 (k1, p1) twice, k1.

Row 8 (inc): K1, p1 (kfb) twice, k2 (8 sts).

Row 9: K1 (k1, p1) 3 times, k1.

Row 10 (inc): K1, p1, k1 (kfb) twice, p1, k2 (10 sts).

Row 11: K1 (k1, p1) 4 times, k1.

Row 12 (inc): (K1, p1) twice (kfb) twice, k1, p1, k2 (12 sts)

Row 13: K1 (k1, p1) twice, p1 (p1, k1) 3 times.

Row 14: (K1, p1) twice, k3 (p1, k1) twice, k1.

Rep Row 13, Row 14, then Row 13 again.

Row 18 (inc): (K1, p1) twice, kfb, k2, kfb, k1, p1, k2 (14 sts).

Row 19: K1 (k1, p1) twice, p4 (k1, p1) twice, k1.

Row 20: (K1, p1) twice, k5 (p1, k1) twice, k1.

Rep Row 19, Row 20, then Row 19 again.

Left side only

Row 24 (buttonhole row): (K1, p1) twice, k5, p1, k1, yf, k2tog, k1.

Right side only

Row 24 (buttonhole row): K1, p1, yf, k2tog, k5, (p1, k1) twice, k1.

Both sides

Row 25: As Row 19.

Row 26 (inc). (K1, p1) twice, kfb, k4, kfb, k1, p1, k2 (16 sts).

Row 27: K1 (k1, p1) twice, p6 (k1, p1) twice, k1.

Row 28: (K1, p1) twice, k7 (p1, k1) twice, k1.

Row 29: As Row 27.

Row 30: As Row 28.

Row 31: As Row 27.

Row 32 (inc): (K1, p1) twice, kfb, k6, kfb, k1, p1, k2 (18 sts).

Row 33: K1 (k1, p1) twice, p8 (k1, p1) twice, k1.

Row 34: (K1, p1) twice, k9 (p1, k1) twice, k1.

Rep Row 33, Row 34, then Row 33 again.

Row 38 (inc): (K1, p1) twice, kfb, k8, kfb, k1, p1, k2 (20 sts).

Row 39: K1 (k1, p1) twice, p10 (k1, p1) twice, k1.

Row 40: (K1, p1) twice, k11 (p1, k1) twice, k1.

Rep Row 33, Row 34, then Row 33 again.

Left side only

Row 44 (inc and buttonhole row): (K1, p1) twice, kfb, k10, kfb, k1, yf, k2tog, k1 (22 sts).

Right side only

Row 44 (inc and buttonhole row): K1, p1, yf, k2tog, kfb, k10, kfb, k1, p1, k2 (22 sts).

Both sides

Row 45: K1 (k1, p1) twice, p12 (k1, p1) twice, k1.

Row 46: (K1, p1) twice, k13 (p1, k1) twice, k1.

Rep Row 45, Row 46, then Row 45 again.

Row 50 (inc): (K1, p1) twice, kfb, k12, kfb, k1, p1, k2 (24 sts).

Row 51: K1 (k1, p1) twice, p14 (k1, p1) twice, k1.

Row 52: (K1, p1) twice, k15 (p1, k1) twice, k1.

Rep Row 51, Row 52, then Row 51 again.

Row 56 (inc): (K1, p1) twice, kfb, k14, kfb, k1, p1, k2 (26 sts).

Row 57: K1 (k1, p1) twice, p16 (k1, p1) twice, k1.

Row 58: (K1, p1) twice, k17 (p1, k1) twice, k1.

Rep Row 57, Row 58, then Row 57 again.

Row 62 (inc): (K1, p1) twice, kfb, k16, kfb, k1, p1, k2 (28 sts).

Row 63: K1 (k1, p1) twice, p18 (k1, p1) twice, k1.

Left side only

Row 64 (buttonhole row): (K1, p1) twice, k19, p1, k1, yf, k2tog, k1.

Right side only

Row 64 (buttonhole row): K1, p1, yf, k2tog, k19 (p1, k1) twice, k1.

Both sides

Row 65: Row 63.

Row 66: (K1, p1) twice, k19 (p1, k1) twice, k1.

Row 67: As Row 63.

Row 68 (inc): (K1, p1) twice, kfb, k18, kfb, k1, p1, k2 (30 sts).

Row 69: K1 (k1, p1) twice, p20 (k1, p1) twice, k1.

Row 70: (K1, p1) twice, k21 (p1, k1) twice, k1.

Rep Row 69, Row 70, then Row 69 again.

Row 80 (inc): (K1, p1) twice, kfb, k22, kfb, k1, p1, k2 (34 sts).

Row 81: K1 (k1, p1) twice, p24 (k1, p1) twice, k1.

Row 82: (K1, p1) twice, k25 (p1, k1) twice, k1.

Row 83: As Row 81.

Left side only

Row 84 (buttonhole row): (K1, p1) twice, k25, p1, k1, yf, k2tog, k1.

Right side only

Row 84 (buttonhole row): K1, p1, yf, k2tog, k25 (p1, k1) twice, k1.

Both sides

Row 85: As Row 81.

Row 86 (inc): (K1, p1) twice, kfb, k24, kfb, k1, p1, k2 (36 sts).

Row 87: K1 (k1, p1) twice, p26 (k1, p1) twice, k1.

Row 88: (K1, p1) twice, k27 (p1, k1) twice, k1.

Rep row 87, Row 88, then Row 87 again.

Row 92 (inc): (K1, p1) twice, kfb, k26, kfb, k1, p1, k2 (38 sts).

Row 93: K1 (k1, p1) twice, p28 (k1, p1) twice, k1.

Row 94: (K1, p1) twice, k29 (p1, k1) twice, k1.

Rep Row 93, Row 94, then Row 93 again.

Row 98 (inc): (K1, p1) twice, kfb, k28, kfb, k1, p1, k2 (40 sts).

Row 99: K1 (k1, p1) twice, p30 (k1, p1) twice, k1.

Row 100: (K1, p1) twice, k31 (p1, k1) twice, k1.

Rep Row 99, Row 100, then Row 99 again.

Left side only

Row 104 (inc and buttonhole row): (K1, p1) twice, kfb, k30, kfb, k1, yf, k2tog, k1 (42 sts).

Right side only

Row 104 (inc and buttonhole row): K1, p1, yf, k2tog, kfb, k30, kfb, k1, p1, k2 (42 sts).

Both sides

Row 105: K1 (k1, p1) twice, p32 (k1, p1) twice, k1.

Row 106: (K1, p1) twice, k33 (p1, k1) twice, k1.

Rep Row 105, Row 106, then Row 105 again.

Row 110 (inc): (K1, p1) twice, kfb, k32, kfb, k1, p1, k2 (44 sts).

Row 111: K1 (k1, p1) twice, p34 (k1, p1) twice, k1.

Row 112: (K1, p1) twice, k35 (p1, k1) twice, k1.

Rep Row 111, Row 112, then Row 111 again.

Row 116 (inc): (K1, p1) twice, kfb, k34, kfb, k1, p1, k2 (46 sts).

Row 117: K1 (k1, p1) twice, p36 (k1, p1) twice, k1.

Row 118: (K1, p1) twice, k37 (p1, k1) twice, k1.

Rep Row 117, Row 118, then Row 117 again.

Row 122 (inc): (K1, p1) twice, kfb, k36, kfb, k1, p1, k2 (48 sts).

Row 123: K1 (k1, p1) twice, p38 (k1, p1) twice, k1.

Left side only

Row 124 (buttonhole row): (K1, p1) twice, k39, p1, k1, yf, k2tog, k1.

Right side only

Row 124 (buttonhole row): K1, p1, yf, k2tog, k39 (p1, k1) twice, k1.

Both sides:

Row 125: K1 (k1, p1) twice, p38 (k1, p1) twice, k1.

Row 126: (K1, p1) twice, k39 (p1, k1) twice, k1.

Rep Row 125, Row 126, then Row 125 again.

Row 130: (K1, p1) to last 2 sts, k2.

Row 131: K1 (k1, p1) to last st, k1.

Rep Rows 130 and 131 twice more. Cast off in pattern.

Finishing

Slipstitch top 5 sts of side button bands to behind buttonhole bands at underarms of each side.

Sew buttons onto button bands, matching buttonholes on body sides and side panels.

Sew in all loose ends neatly.

HINTS AND TIPS

- You can work the whole sweater on a 3.75 mm circular needle if you use the magic loop method (see page 93). Otherwise you will also need double-pointed needles or a smaller-circumference circular needle to work the sleeves.

- You can shorten or lengthen the sweater by adding or subtracting 2 rows between each buttonhole.

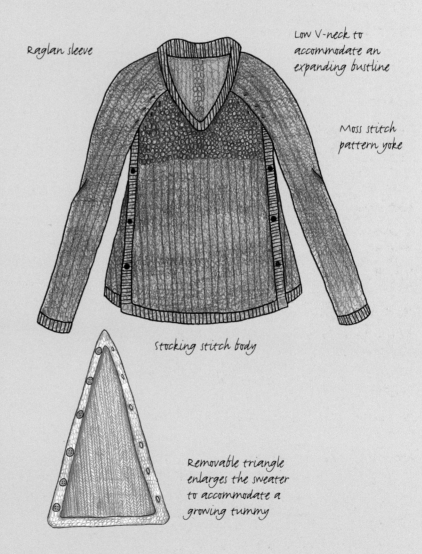

Raglan sleeve

Low V-neck to accommodate an expanding bustline

Moss stitch pattern yoke

Stocking stitch body

Removable triangle enlarges the sweater to accommodate a growing tummy

SEACHANGE SWEATER
Organic Gansey to anchor links with a friend
by Julia Hopson

There will be times when you want to give a friend a sweater that symbolizes finding safe harbour – whether she is setting off on a journey or is at difficult time in her life. This design is an adaptation of the traditional Cornish Gansey, made for sailors. The pattern is called 'Eddystone', after the lighthouse near the harbour of Looe. Originally, each harbour had its own pattern so that if a fisherman was washed overboard his body could be returned to the right village.

Cornish Ganseys were traditionally knitted in the round in oiled 5-ply wool, and were very fitted to ensure maximum warmth and waterproofing. This pattern is worked in double-knit Cornish Organic Wool and is less fitted, in keeping with modern fashions. The bottom welt is garter stitch and this can be left open when stitching up if you want a vent. The body pieces are worked on two needles, but the shoulder seams and neck are worked in the traditional way by knitting the front and back seams together on three needles, adding the neck and completing in the round. Sleeves are worked on two needles and a traditional underarm gusset is worked at the top of each sleeve. Often, initials would be worked into the gussets by knitting in reverse stocking stitch to identify the wearer. Initials can be worked into the gussets of your Seachange Sweater for a personal touch!

ABBREVIATIONS

K knit
P purl
St(s) stitch(es)
WS wrong side
RS right side
Inc increase
Beg beginning

GLOSSARY

Garter stitch: Knit every row
Stocking stitch: 1 row knit, 1 row purl

KNITTING THE SWEATER

Knitting the Body (Make 2)

Using 4 mm needles, cast on 88 [94, 98, 110, 120] sts.

Work 18 rows in garter stitch.

Work 6 rows in k2, p2 rib.

Starting with a k row, continue in stocking stitch until work measures 35 cm (14 ins) or desired length.

Commence Eddystone Lighthouse pattern:

Row 1: K7 [5, 7, 7, 7], (p7, k4) 6 [7, 7, 8, 9] times, p7, k8 [5, 7, 8, 7].

Row 2 and every alternate row: Purl.

Row 3: K8 [6, 8, 8, 8], (p5, k6) 6 [7, 7, 8, 9] times, p5, k9 [6, 8, 9, 8].

Row 5: K9 [7, 9, 9, 9] (p3, k8) 6 [7, 7, 8, 9] times, p3, k10 [7, 9, 10, 9].

Rows 7 and 9: K10 [8, 10, 10, 10], (p1, k10) 6 [7, 7, 8, 9] times, p1, k11 [8, 10, 11, 10].

Rows 11–14: Work in stocking stitch.

Knit 3 [4, 4, 4, 5] cm (1 [1½, 1½, 1½, 2] ins) of pattern, ending with a purl row.

Place a marker at each end of this row (this marks the underarm).

Continue in pattern until the depth of the armhole (from markers) is 23 [24, 25.5, 26.5, 28] cm (9 [9½, 10, 10½, 11] ins).

Transfer stitches to a stitch holder until ready to join two sides together.

MATERIALS

Yarn
4 [5, 5, 6, 6] 100 g skeins Cornish Organic Wool DK

Needles
2 pairs 4 mm needles
1 x 4 mm 40-cm (16-in) circular needle or 1 set double-pointed needles
Stitch holders

SIZE

Bust: 86 [91, 96.5, 101.5, 112] cm (34 [36, 38, 40, 44] ins)

Actual measurement: 90 [95, 100, 105, 115.5] cm (35½ [37½, 39½, 41½, 45½] ins)

Length from back neck: 61 [63, 64.5, 65.5, 68] cm (24 [25, 25¼, 25¾, 26¾] ins)

Figures in square brackets [] refer to the larger sizes. Where only one figure is given this refers to all sizes.

TENSION

19 sts and 26 rows over 10 cm (4 ins)

Join the 2 body pieces:
Place the 2 pieces together, wrong sides facing, take 1 st from the front and 1 st from the back and knit them together and cast off.
Repeat until 24 [26, 28, 32, 34] sts have been cast off.

Making the neck gussets
With 1 st on the right-hand needle (from casting off), restore the needles holding the work to their 'proper' knitting position, i.e. front to the left, back to the right.

1st Row: K1 from the front, turn.

2nd Row: *P these 2 sts and 1 from the back (3 sts), turn.

3rd Row: K these 3 sts and 1 from the front (4 sts), turn.

Continue in this way until there are 9 sts.

Turn and knit across the gusset and front to last 24 [26, 28, 32, 34] sts. Cast off the second shoulder as for the first.

Rejoin yarn and work the second gusset as the first.

Knit across the back of the gansey to the first gusset.

With the circular needle, continue knitting in the round in k2, p2 rib until neck measures 4 cm (1½ ins).

Cast off loosely in rib.

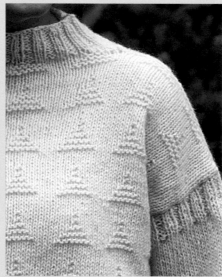

Knitting the Sleeves

Using 4 mm needles, cast on 50 [52, 52, 52, 52] sts.

Work in k2, p2 rib for 8 cm (3 ins), ending with a ws row.

Work in stocking stitch for 5 rows.

Next row and every following 5 rows: Continuing in stocking stitch, inc 1 st in the 2nd st from beg and 2nd st from end of next row and every following 5 rows until there are 68 [76, 84, 86, 88] sts.

Continue without shaping until work measures 42 [42, 44, 44, 45] cm (16½ [16½, 17, 17, 17¾] ins) from cast-on edge.

Armhole gusset

Cast on 12 sts at beg of next row. Work in stocking stitch for 2 cm (¾ in), ending with a WS row.

Work in k2, p2 rib for 3 cm (1 in), but continue the gusset in stocking stitch.

Cast off in rib/stocking stitch.

Finishing

To sew in the sleeves, place the centre of the sleeve ribbed section to the shoulder seam. Set in the sleeve and gusset. Sew in the sleeve and gusset.

Sew up the side and sleeve seams. The bottom of each side seam (below the rib) can be left open if a vent is desired.

Press your gansey gently.

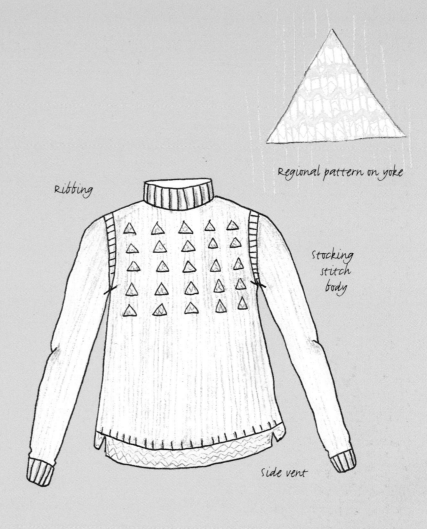

Regional pattern on yoke

Ribbing

stocking stitch body

side vent

HINTS AND TIPS

- For a firm, neat edge to side openings, slip the first stitch from each row from left to right needle without working it.

- Organic yarn is best given a gentle handwash, adding a spoonful of baby oil to the final rinse, If desired, to keep the 'oiled' feel of the wool.

MATERIALS

Yarn

2 x 100 g skeins of Knitwitches Superwash Sock Yarn (4-ply weight) (Yarn A)

1 x 100 g skein of Knitwitches Superwash Sock Yarn (4-ply weight) in contrasting colour (Yarn B)

Needles

1 pair 3.25 mm needles

1 pair 3.75 mm needles

1 x 3.25 mm circular needle

1 set 3.25 mm double-pointed needles or 2 x 3.25 mm circular needles (optional)

Stitch holders

TENSION

24 sts and 31 rows over 10 cm (4 ins) over pattern on 3.75 mm needles

MEASUREMENTS

Bust: 86 [96, 106] cm (34 [38, 42] ins)

Figures in square brackets [] refer to larger sizes. Where only one figure is given this refers to all sizes.

ABBREVIATIONS

K knit
P purl
St(s) stitch(es)
K2tog knit 2 stitches together
YO yarn over – wrap yarn around needle to create a stitch (see Glossary for detailed instructions)
Sl1, k1, psso Slip 1, knit 1, pass the slipped stitch over (see Glossary for detailed instructions).

GLOSSARY

YO NB. When using YO between 2 knit stitches, bring the yarn to the front of the work. When using YO from a knit to a purl stitch or from a purl to a knit stitch, wind the yarn around the needle so that a new stitch is formed; one will be from the back to the front of the work and the other will be from the front to the back of the work.

Sl1, k1, psso Slip 1 stitch onto right-hand needle without knitting, knit 1 stitch; using left-hand needle, pick up slipped stitch and pass over knitted stitch.

KNITTING THE TANK TOP
Back

Using 3.25 mm needles and Yarn B, cast on 106 [116, 126] sts.

1st Row: Break off Yarn B and attach Yarn A, k2, p2 across row to last 2 [0, 2] sts, k2 [k0, k2].

Next Row: P2 [p0, p2], (k2, p2) to end.

Repeat these 2 rows until work measures 13 cm (5 ins).*

Change to 3.75 mm needles and work in stocking stitch until work measures 30 [30, 33] cm (12 [12, 13] ins) or desired length to armhole.

LOVING LACE TANK TOP
Heartwarming slipover for a friend who feels the cold
by Eirwen Godfrey and Sue Hawkins

Quicker to knit than a jumper, this lace-panel slipover will bring a really welcome touch of warmth without weight to the recipient. Eirwen used sock yarn for this project to show its versatility – the majority of sock yarn is merely a 4-ply weight yarn, so you can use it for so many other purposes apart from keeping toes cosy.

The top finishes at the hip. If your friend needs more coverage to keep her warm, and so you need the tank top to be longer, then merely increase the length you knit to the armhole.

Armhole shaping

Continuing in stocking stitch, cast off 5 sts at the beginning of next 2 rows (96 [106, 116] sts).

Decrease Row: K3, (sl1, k1, psso), k to last 5 sts, k2tog, k3.

Next Row: P.

Repeat the last two rows 4 more times (86 [96, 106] sts).

Then repeat the decrease row every 4th row 7 times (72 [82, 92] sts).

Continue in stocking stitch until armhole measures 21 [23, 23] cm (8 [9, 9] ins), finishing on a wrong side row.

Shoulder shaping

Cast off 9 [10, 13] sts at start of next 2 rows.

Cast off 10 [11, 13] sts at the start of following 2 rows.

Place remaining 34 [40, 40] sts onto a stitch holder and break yarn.

Knitting the Front

Work as for back to *.
Change to 3.75 mm needles.

NB. Please check Glossary for working of YO on each row.

Row 1: K36 [41, 46], p5, k3, k2tog, k4, yo, p2, yo, k2tog, p2, yo, k4, sl1, k1, psso, k3, p5, k36 [41, 46].

Row 2: P36 [41, 46], k5, p9, k2, p2, k2, p9, k5, p36 [41, 46].

Row 3: K 36 [41, 46], p5, k2, k2tog, k4, yo, k1, p2, k2tog, yo, p2, k1, yo, k4, sl1, k1, psso, k2, p5, k36 [41, 46].

Row 4: As Row 2.

Row 5: K 36 [41, 46], p5, k1, k2tog, k4, yo, k2, p2, yo, k2tog, p2, k2, yo, k4, sl1, k1, psso, k1, p5, k36 [41, 46].

Row 6: As Row 2.

Row7: K 36 [41, 46], p5, k2tog, k4, yo, k3, p2, k2tog, yo, p2, k3, yo, k4, sl1, k1, psso, p5, k36 [41, 46].

Row 8: As Row 2.

These 8 rows form the pattern.

Repeat the pattern until work measures the same as the back to the armhole, finishing on a wrong side row.

Armhole and neck shaping

Cast off 5 sts, k 31 [36, 41], p5, k9, p2, k2, turn, leaving remaining stitches on a stitch holder.

Next Row: Cast off 2 sts (it is important to keep tension tight when casting off these sts), k2, p9, k5, p to end.

Next Row: K3, sl1, k1, psso, k26 [31, 36], p5, k7, k2tog, p2.

Next Row: K2, p8, k5, p to end.

Note: On right side rows work p2 and on wrong side rows work k2 at neck edge.

* Continuing in pattern as set, repeat last 2 rows 4 more times (40, [45, 50] sts).

Decrease 1 st at armhole edge every 4th row 7 times and AT THE SAME TIME decrease 1 st at neck edge on alternate rows 6 [8, 13] times and then every 4th row 4 [3, 0] times (19 [21, 26] sts).

Continue in pattern as set until work measures the same as for back, finishing on a wrong side row.

Cast off 9 [10, 13] sts.

Work one row.

Cast off remaining 10 [11, 13] sts.

Left-hand side of neck shaping

Place sts from stitch holder onto needles.

With right side facing, rejoin Yarn A at neck edge and p2, k9, p5, k31.

Next Row: Cast off 5 [5, 5] sts, p31 [36, 41], k5, p9, k2.

Next Row: (Neck edge) p2, (sl1, k1, psso, k7, p5, k26 [31, 36], k2tog, k3.

Next Row: P30 [35, 40], k5, p8, k2.

Work as for right-hand side of neck from *, working one extra row before starting to cast off.

Finishing

Block the 2 pieces of the tank top so that they are flat, and allow to dry.

Sew the side seams and the shoulder seams together. Sew in all the loose ends.

Working the Neckband

With the right side facing, with a 3.25 mm circular needle and Yarn A k34 [40, 40] sts from the back stitch holder, then evenly pick up and k49 [55, 55] sts down the left side of the neck and 49 [55, 55] sts up the right side of the neck (132 [150, 150] sts).

** Place a marker at the start of the round.

Knit 10 rounds.

Attach Yarn B and break off Yarn A.

Cast off using the lace method as follows:

K2, transfer stitches one at a time back to left-hand needle, k2 tog (there should now be 1 st on the righthand needle), k1 (there are now 2 sts on the right-hand needle).

Repeat this process until 1 st remains.

Break yarn and finish off last st.***

Working the Armbands
Use 3.25 mm circular needles.
(**Note**: You may need to use 3.25 mm double-pointed needles for the armholes, as they are smaller than the neck; 2 circular needles may also be used.)

Starting at side seam, with Yarn A evenly pick up and k46 [52, 52] sts along front of armhole, then evenly pick up and k47 [53, 53] sts along back of armhole (93 [106, 106] sts.

Follow the directions for the neckband from ** to ***.

Repeat for second armhole.

Finishing off the neckband and armbands
Turn the bands over so that the reverse stocking stitch side is facing and pin so that the contrast colour cast-off is gently against the edge of the neck where the 2 p sts meet the k sts.

Using a tapestry needle and Yarn B, invisibly hem the band into place along the cast-off edge of the neckband.

Finish the yarn off on the wrong side.

Gently steam iron into place.

Repeat for the armbands.

HINTS AND TIPS

- The tank top shows how effective lace can be as an insert into a garment. The lace insert is a very easy 8-row pattern, with every other row a purl row.

- The yarn was hand dyed especially for the pattern, but you could use any Knitwitches sock yarn. The contrasting colour at the bottom of the tank top and on the neck and armholes is created by using a darker yarn to cast on and then immediately changing to the main yarn for the first row. For the armholes and neck, rejoin the darker yarn at the cast-off row and use it for casting off.

- To gain a softer, looser edge for casting off, use a lace cast off (full details of how to do this are given in the pattern).

- If you need the Tank Top longer, then merely increase the length to the armhole.

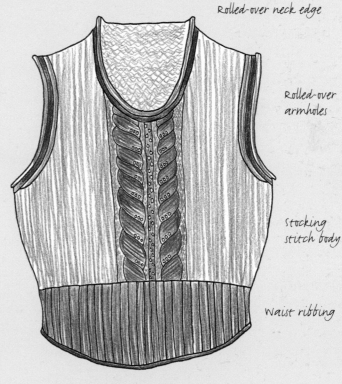

Rolled-over neck edge

Rolled-over armholes

stocking stitch body

Waist ribbing

Lace cable pattern

A SCARF FOR BAD HAIR DAYS
Stylish cover-up for hair issues of any kind
by Sue Hawkins

A versatile head scarf which can be worn in different ways (see Hints and Tips) and could be made for a woman experiencing hair loss. Whether her hair loss is due to treatment for cancer or another medical reason, the scarf will be warmly received. The Seriously Gorgeous cashmere and silk yarn really lives up to its name by supplying luxury, comfort and style. The comfort will be needed in extra measure if the person you make this for is undergoing treatment for cancer as her scalp will be extra-sensitive.

MATERIALS

Yarn
1 x 100 g hank Knitwitches Seriously Gorgeous Cashmere and Silk Mix

Other Materials
Approximately 50 x 10 mm (30 count) beads for the scarf and flower pin

Note: Beads are optional. If used, put them on alternate drops on the scarf or on every drop (this will require more beads)

Safety pin

Needles
1 pair 4 mm needles

SIZE
Drop: 55 cm (21½ ins)
Width: 100 cm (39 ins)

This size is suitable for wearing over the head; if you prefer a shawl, knit it longer – quantity of yarn given should be enough for approximately 18 cm (7 ins) extra.

TENSION
18 sts and 36 rows over 10 cm (4 ins) over pattern on 4 mm needles

ABBREVIATIONS
K knit
P purl
St(s) stitch(es)
PB place bead (use the crochet hook method or thread them on the yarn before knitting)

KFB knit into the front and back of stitch (increases by one)

YO yarn over needle (k 1st st, bring yarn to front between 2 needle points and k next st – the yarn has formed a loop over the needle between the 2 sts)

KNITTING THE HEADSCARF

Cast on 1 st, pb, cast on 1 st (2 sts).

(K 1 row, p 1 row) 3 times (6 rows worked).

Next Row: KFB twice.

Next Row: K1 (kfb) twice, k1.

Next Row: K2 (kfb) twice, k2.

Commence pattern:

Row 1: K3, p to last 3 sts, k3.

Row 2: K3, yo, k to last 3 sts, yo, k3.

Row 3: Cast on 5, pb, cast off 5, k to end.

Row 4: Cast on 5, pb, cast off 5, k2, yo, k to last 3 sts, yo, k3.

Row 5: K3, p to last 3 sts, k3.

Row 6: K3, yo, k to last 3 sts, yo, k3.

Row 7: K.

Row 8: K3, yo, k to last 3 sts, yo, k3.

Repeat these 8 rows, ending on Row 4 (182 sts and 22 drops on each side).

K 1 row.

Cast off 3 (cast on 5, pb, cast off 5, cast off 8) 16 times, cast on 5, pb, cast off 8.

FLOWER PIN

Knitting the Outer Petal

Cast on 12 sts.

* Cast off 8 sts, k4, turn, k4, cast on 8 sts, repeat from * 18 times.

Cast off 8 sts, k4, cast off 4 sts (19 drops).

Sew up cast-off and cast-on edges to make a circle.

Knitting the Inner Petal

Cast on 9 sts.

*Cast off 6 sts, k3, turn, k3 sts, cast on 6 sts, repeat from * 25 times.

Cast off 6 sts, k3, cast off 3 sts (26 drops).

Gather up along knitted edge into a circle.

Sew the two petals together, attach beads to the centre (if required) and sew onto a safety pin.

HINTS AND TIPS

- Experiment with different ways of tying the headscarf – under the chin, at the back of the neck or turban style. On a good hair day it can be worn at the neck.

- You can embellish the scarf by the addition of the knitted flower.

- You may choose not to include the beaded tassels on the edge of the scarf. If you want to leave them out then simply remove the following from the third and fourth rows – cast on 5, pb, cast off 5.

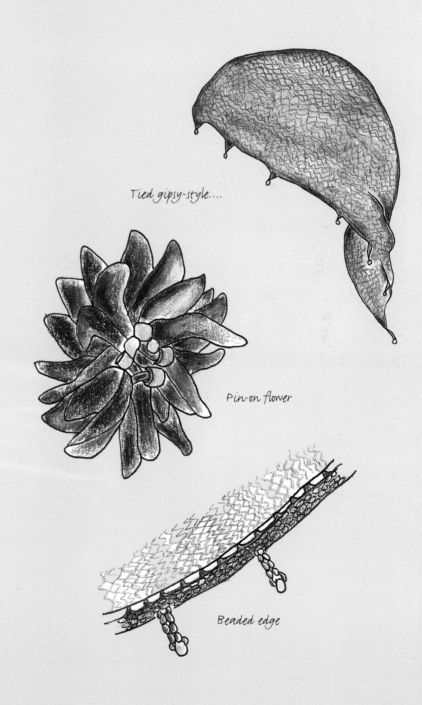

Tied gipsy-style....

Pin-on flower

Beaded edge

PAMPER WITH A BERET & NECK WRAP
Treat a friend with soft, sustainable cashmere

by Julie Prior

Julie tells me she has a friend who spoils everyone except herself. She's there, first to help when you are in trouble and the last to criticise when you foul up! Hugs and laughter plus a good dash of homespun wisdom when you ask for it make her the perfect soulmate.

Apart from her friends, her other passion is the natural world and the disastrous effect we humans are having on it. Always ready to live her beliefs, she has given up wearing and eating so many things because of the way they are farmed that finding treats for her, little things to make her feel good and say thank you, is getting harder by the year.

Fortunately, she will still wear Julie's Devon cashmere. Unlike Chinese or Inner Mongolian cashmere, it causes no environmental damage during production or processing. On Julie's farm in the south-west of England the animals and the land we share with them are treated with kindness and respect at all times. The goats live an idyllic life in beautiful surroundings and reward us with the softest, highest quality cashmere that Julie processes in England, which has some of the toughest environmental legislation in the world. Julie feels it is her privilege to share the lives of her animals and to use the fibre they produce.

This beret and neck wrap are Julie's thank you for the love and companionship of her friend and a recognition of her concern for the world we all share.

Knitting the Beret

Using Yarn A and 2.75 mm double-pointed needles, cast on 140 sts and distribute evenly over the 4 needles. Place marker at the end of cast-on row and join to beginning, ensuring that the stitches do not become twisted.

Knit 15 rounds in 1x1 rib, i.e. k1, p1 for all rounds.

Increase row

K2, make 1. Repeat to end of row (210 sts).

Change to 3 mm needles and using Yarns A and B as indicated, work as follows:

Yarn A. 1st Round. K1, *wyaf sl3, k3, repeat from * to end of round.

Yarn B. 2nd Round. K1, *wyaf sl1, k5, repeat from * to last 4 sts, k4.

Yarn B. 3rd Round. K1, *wyaf sl1, k5, repeat from * to last 4 sts, k4.

Yarn A. 4th Round. K1, * insert left needle down behind loose Yarn A strand of Round 1, lift over point of left needle and k2tog (i.e. the Yarn A strand and the first Yarn B st on the needle), repeat from * to last 4 sts, k4.

Yarn A. 5th Round. *K3, wyaf sl3, repeat from * to end of round.

Yarn B. 6th Round. K4, *wyif sl1, k5, repeat from * to last 2 sts, wyaf sl1, k1.

Yarn B. 7th Round. K4, *wyif sl1, k5, repeat from * to last 2 sts, wyaf sl1, k1.

Yarn A. 8th Round. K4, *insert left needle down behind loose Yarn A strand of Round 5, lift over point of left needle and k2tog (i.e. the Yarn A strand and the 1st Yarn B st on needle), repeat from * to last st, k1.

These 8 rounds form the pattern. Continue until 6 pattern repeats have been completed. Work should measure 11.5 cm (4½ ins).

Cut off Yarn B. Use Yarn A only to finish.

MATERIALS

Yarn

Neck wrap: 25 g 4-ply (fingering weight) Devon cashmere in colour A (Yarn A) 15 g 4-ply (fingering weight) Devon cashmere in colour B (Yarn B)

Beret: 20 g 4-ply (fingering weight) Devon cashmere in colour A (Yarn A) 25 g 4-ply (fingering weight) Devon cashmere colour B (Yarn B)

Needles

Neck wrap: 1 pair 3 mm needles
Beret: 1 set each of 2.75 mm and 3 mm double-pointed needles

TENSION

10 sts and 12 rows over 4 cm (1½ ins)

ABBREVIATIONS

K knit
P purl
St(s) stitch(es)
St st stocking stitch
Sl slip
Wyab with yarn at back of work
Wyaf with yarn at front of work
Tog together

Decrease rounds

1st Decrease Round. *K3, k2tog, repeat from * to end.

Knit 11 rounds in st st.

2nd Decrease Round. *K2, k2tog, repeat from * to end.

Knit 8 rounds in st st.

3rd Decrease Round. *K1, k2tog, repeat from * to end.

Knit 8 rounds in st st.

4th Decrease Round. *k2tog, repeat from * to end.

Knit 5 rounds in st st.

5th Decrease Round. *k2tog, repeat from * to end.

Change to 2.75 mm needles

6th Decrease Round. *k2tog, repeat from * to last 3 sts, k3tog.

Cut yarn and thread through remaining sts. Pull tight and fasten to inside.

Finishing

Block beret by cutting a circle of cardboard to just stretch the pattern so that all wrinkles are smoothed. Spritz the beret lightly with water and allow to dry naturally. Remove cardboard.

Knitting the Neck Wrap

Using Yarn A, cast on 48 sts.
Knit 3 rows in moss stitch as follows:
1st Row: K1, p1 to end.

2nd Row: P1, k1 to end.

3rd Row: K1, p1 to end.

Working the Pattern

1st Row: P1, k1, p1 *with yarn at back of work, sl3, p3, repeat from * to last 3 sts, k1, p1, k1.

2nd Row: K1, p1, k1, with Yarn B *k4, with yarn at front of work, s11, k1, repeat from * to last 3 sts, in Yarn A, p1, k1, p1.

3rd Row: With Yarn A, p1, k1, p1, in Yarn B, *p1, wyab sl1, p4, repeat from * to last 3 sts, with Yarn A, k1, p1, k1.

4th Row: With Yarn A, k1, p1, k1, still working with Yarn A, * k4, insert left needle point down behind loose colour A of Row 1, lift this strand over point of left-hand needle and k2tog (i.e. the Yarn A strand and the 1st stitch on the left needle), k1, repeat from * to last 4 sts, k1, p1, k1, p1.

5th Row: With Yarn A, p1, k1, p1, *p3, wyab sl3, repeat from * to last 3 sts, k1, p1, k1.

6th Row: With Yarn A, k1, p1, k1, with Yarn B, *k1, wyaf sl1, k4, repeat from * to last 3 sts, with Yarn A, p1, k1, p1.

7th Row: With Yarn A, p1, k1, p1, with Yarn B, *p4, wyib sl1, p1, repeat from * to last 3 sts, with Yarn A, k1, p1, k1.

8th Row: With Yarn A, k1, p1, k1, *k1, insert left needle down behind loose Yarn A of Row 5, lift over point of left needle and k2tog (i.e. the loose Yarn A strand and the 1st st on the needle), k4, repeat from * to last 3 sts, p1, k1, p1.

These 8 rows form the pattern.
Continue for 6 pattern repeats.

Cut off Yarn B.

Keeping the 3-st edge at each side, continue in st st with Yarn A until work measures 50 cm (18¾ ins).

Work 6 pattern repeats in the same way as the first end of the scarf.

Using Yarn A, work 3 rows in moss stitch as follows:

1st Row: K1, p1.

2nd Row: P1, k1.

3rd Row: K1,p1.

Cast off in moss stitch.

Finishing
Neatly sew in all loose ends.

HINTS AND TIPS

- If you want to make a longer, wrap-around scarf, then just simply double the number of rows you knit for the unpatterned section of the neckwrap.
- Handwash delicate fibres like this fine cashmere in a pure liquid detergent especially designed for pure wools – and please make sure that the product is eco-friendly, in the spirit of the yarn!

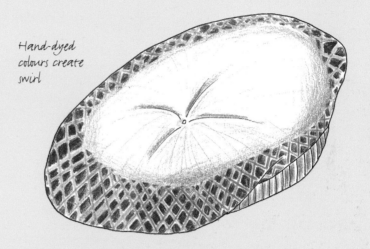

Hand-dyed colours create swirl

simple slipstitch pattern

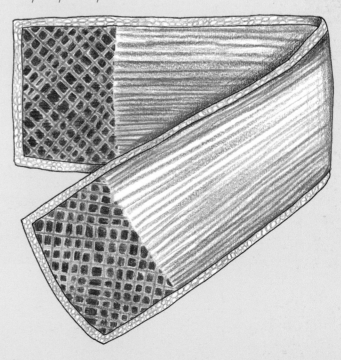

Moss-stitch border helps keep scarf flat

MATERIALS

Yarn
1 skein any sock weight yarn (e.g. Cherry Tree Hill Supersock)

Needles
1 set 2.25 mm double-pointed needles
6 stitch markers
Tapestry needle for grafting

Note: It is assumed in this pattern that you will know where each row starts and ends.

TENSION
8.5 sts and 13 rows over 2.5 cm (1 in)

SIZE
To fit adult size 5-6 (adjustable)

ABBREVIATIONS
K knit
P purl
St(s) stitch(es)
PM place marker
K2tog knit 2 together
Tbl through back of loop
SSM slip stitch marker
SSPW slip stitch purlwise
Sl slip
Dec decrease(ing)

3st-RPC = slip 1 stitch onto cable needle and hold at back, knit two stitches, purl stitch from cable needle.

3st-LPC= slip 2 stitches onto cable needle and hold at front, purl one stitch, knit two stitches from cable needle.

C4B= slip 2 stitches onto cable needle and hold at back, knit 2, knit 2 from cable needle.

C4F= slip 2 stitches onto cable needle and hold at front, knit 2 stitches, knit 2 stitches from cable needle.

KNITTING THE SOCKS

Cast on 76 sts using cable cast on (or your preferred) method.

Join to knit in the round, being careful not to twist sts.

Divide sts evenly between needles (19 sts on each if using 5 double-pointed needles).

Row 1: P1, k2, p2, k2, p2, k2, pm, p2, k2, p2, k4, p2, k2, p2, k2, p2, pm, k2, p2, k2, p2, k2, p2, k2, pm, p2, k2, p2, k2, p2, k4, p2, k2, p2, pm, k2, p2, k2, p2, k2, p1.

Repeat this row 19 more times, or until ribbing is desired length.

Pattern set up row: (this row involves decreasing 4 sts to take stitch count down to 72 overall). P1, k2, p2, k2, p2, k2, ssm, p4, p2tog, k4, p6, k2, p2, ssm, k3, k2tog tbl, k4, k2tog, k3, ssm, p2, k2, p6, k4, p2tog, p4, ssmk2, p2, k2, p2, k2, p1.

There should now be 72 sts (18 sts on each needle on 4 double-pointed needles).

Knitting the Cuff
K11 (work Row 1 from Chart A), k12 (work Row 1 from Chart B), k11.

Using the charts, continue in pattern, working 2 repeats of the 24-row pattern and the beginning of a third repeat, ending on Row 13.

Note: If desired, the cuff may be made longer by adding in an extra pattern repeat, but you must still do that extra half-pattern repeat and end on Row 13 of the charts for the heel pattern to work.

LONG & WINDING ROAD WALKER'S SOCKS
Crafty cables for a charity walker
by Melissa Williams

As a gift or thank you for someone who walks or runs a lot, socks are a given. Sore, tired or overworked feet need all the love they can get, and a pair of hand-knit socks that have been especially designed for them is all the love they need.

Melissa has created a perfect cable design that twists in and out of itself at regular intervals, perfectly mimicking the route or journey that a marathon might follow. The twist and curve of the cable is not too taxing for the knitter and it looks great as it opens up and travels up the leg. So, on your marks, get set, KNIT!

A

24
23
21
22
20
19
18
17
16
15
14
13
12
11
10
9
8
7
6
5
4
3
2
1

B

24
23
21
22
20
19
18
17
16
15
14
13
12
11
10
9
8
7
6
5
4
3
2
1

☐ Knit

• Purl

Cable 1 over left

Cable 1 over right

Cable 2 over left

Cable 2 over right

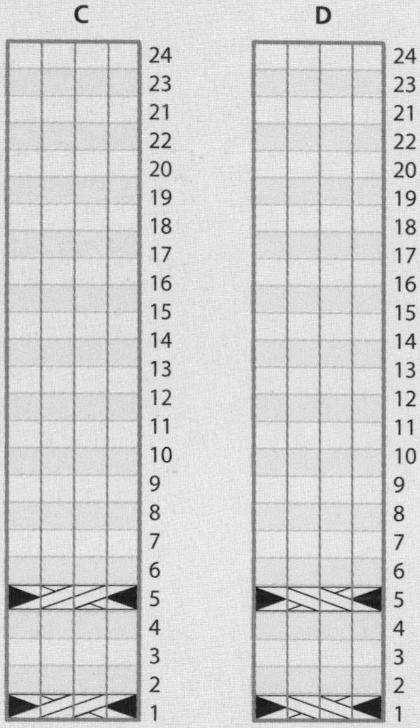
C
D
24
23
21
22
20
19
18
17
16
15
14
13
12
11
10
9
8
7
6
5
4
3
2
1

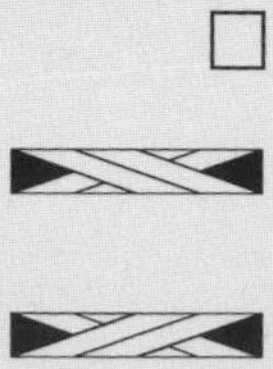
Knit
C4F
Cable 2 over left
C4B
Cable 2 over right

Knitting the Heel Flap

K12, p2, k2, p2, place next 36 sts onto stitch holder or spare needles, turn and work heel flap over remaining 32 sts.

Row 1: Sspw1, then continue to knit across heel flap, knitting all k sts and purling all p sts, turn.

Row 2: Sspw1, p2, k2, p2, (k1, sl1) 11 times, p2, k2, p3.

Repeat these two rows 15 more times, or until heel flap is the correct length to fit your foot, ending with right side facing.

Turning the Heel

Row 1: K21, k2tog tbl, k1, turn.

Row 2: Sl1, p7, p2tog, p1, turn.

Row 3: Sl1, k to 1 st before gap, k2tog tbl, k1, turn.

Row 4: Sl1, p to 1 st before gap, p2tog, p1, turn.

Continue in this way until all heel flap stitches have been worked. There should now be 22 sts left from the heel flap.

Knitting the Gussets

Pick up 18 sts (see note below) along side of heel flap (if you increased the length of the heel flap earlier, you will need to pick up extra sts accordingly), pm.

Note: Pick up the st, then k into it through the back loop to form a twisted stitch; this eliminates any little holes and looks neat .

Transfer the 36 instep sts onto needles and work across these, knitting all k sts and purling all p sts, pm.

Pick up 18 sts (or appropriate number) on other side of heel flap, k 11 sts.There should now be 36 instep sts and 58 sts from the heel flap.

K one round in pattern.

Next Round: K27 (up to 2 sts before stitch marker), k2tog, ssm, p3, k4, p5, k12, p5, k4, p3, ssm, k2tog tbl, k27.

Next Round: Work in pattern.

Next Round: K26, k2tog, ssm, p3, k4, p5, k12, p5, k4, p3, ssm, k2tog tbl, k26.

Next Round: Work in pattern.

Next Round: K25, k2tog, ssm, p3, k4, p5, k12, p5, k4, p3, ssm, k2tog tbl, k25.

Continue in pattern, dec 1 st every 2 rows until there are 78 sts in total (36 instep sts, 42 foot sts).

Next Round: K20, ssm, p3, work Row 1 from Chart C, p5, k12, p5, work Row 1 from Chart D, p3, ssm, k to end of row.

Next Round: K to 2 sts before marker, k2tog, ssm, p3, work Row 2 of Chart C, p5, k12, p5, work Row 2 of Chart D, p3, ssm, k2tog tbl, k to end of row.

Next Round: K to stitch marker, ssm, p3, work Row 3 from Chart C, p5, k12, p5, work Row 3 from Chart D, p3, ssm, k to end of row.

Next Round: K to 2 sts before marker, K2tog, ssm, p3, work Row 4 of Chart C, p5, k12, p5, work Row 4 of Chart D, p3, ssm, k2tog tbl, k to end of row.

Next Round: K to stitch marker, ssm, p3, work Row 5 from Chart C, p5, k12, p5, work Row 5 from Chart D, p3, ssm, k to end of row.

Note: You should now have decreased to 72 sts overall. If you want the sock to be a snugger fit around the foot, continue to decrease at the end of the gusset, working decreases into the pattern until you have the required size. If you picked up extra sts along the heel flaps you will have more than 72 sts and will need to continue decreasing until you reach 72 sts or the required number.

Knitting the Foot

K to stitch marker, ssm, p3, work Row 6 from Chart C, p5, k12, p5, work Row 6 from Chart D, p3, ssm, k to end of row.

Continue working in this manner, following Charts C and D until sock is 5 cm (2 ins) shorter than the required length.

Knitting the Toe

1st Round: K to 3 sts before stitch marker, k2tog, k1, ssm, k1, k2tog tbl, k to 3 sts before stitch marker, k2tog, k1, ssm, k1, k2tog tbl, k to end of row.

2nd Round: K all sts.

Repeat these two rounds, dec 4 sts every two rounds until there are 24 sts remaining.

K 6 rows.

Place sts onto 2 needles, with 12 sts from top of sock on one needle and 12 sts from sole of sock on the other needle.

Grafting the Toe (Kitchener stitch)

Graft toe tog using following method:

Arrange needles so they are parallel to each other.

Break off yarn, leaving a sizeable tail to graft and weave in ends.

Insert tapestry needle into first st on front needle as if to p, draw yarn up through st.

Insert tapestry needle into first st on back needle as if to k, draw yarn up through st.

These are your two set-up sts.

Proceed as follows:
Step 1. Insert tapestry needle into first st on front needle as if to k, draw yarn through st and drop st off front needle.

Step 2. Insert tapestry needle into first st on front needle as if to purl, draw yarn through and leave st on front needle.

Step 3. Insert tapestry needle into first st on back needle as if to purl, draw yarn through and slip st off back needle.

Step 4. Insert tapestry needle into first st on back needle as if to knit, draw yarn through but leave st on back needle.

Repeat these 4 steps until all sts are grafted. Pull yarn through last st to secure. Weave in ends to complete sock.

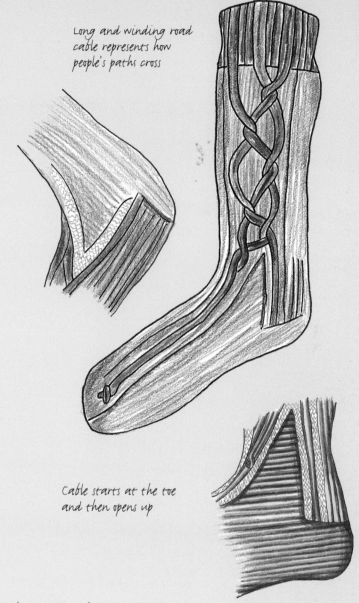

Long and winding road cable represents how people's paths cross

Cable starts at the toe and then opens up

HINTS AND TIPS

- For the magic loop method use one long circular needle, cast on, divide stitches in half and arrange half of the stitches on each end of the needle (the 'home' posiition). To knit, pull the needle so that the back stitches slide onto the loop and knit the stitches from the front needle onto the back needle. When you reach the end of the front needle, turn sock around, push the stitches from the loop onto the new front needle and start over.

- If you want the sock to be a snugger fit around the foot, you will need to continue to decrease at the end of the gusset, working decreases into the pattern until you have the required size.

For Men to Prize

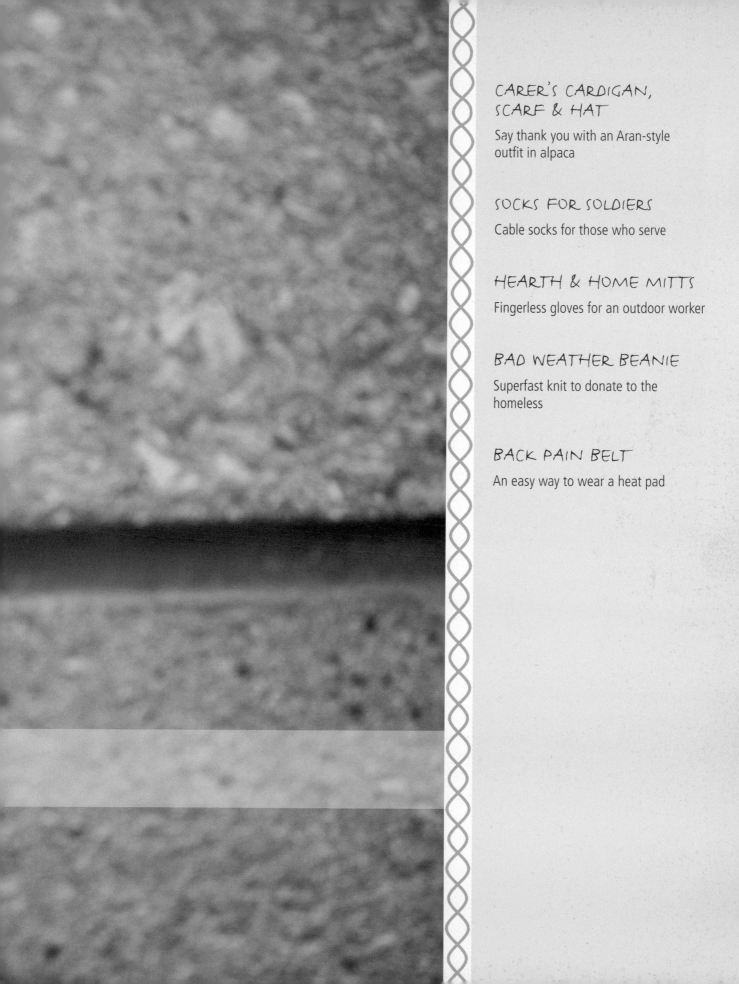

CARER'S CARDIGAN, SCARF & HAT

Say thank you with an Aran-style outfit in alpaca

SOCKS FOR SOLDIERS

Cable socks for those who serve

HEARTH & HOME MITTS

Fingerless gloves for an outdoor worker

BAD WEATHER BEANIE

Superfast knit to donate to the homeless

BACK PAIN BELT

An easy way to wear a heat pad

CARER'S CARDIGAN, SCARF & HAT
Say thank you with an Aran-style outfit in alpaca
by Sue Hanmore

Do you have a male friend who cares for a sick relative, works as a carer for a living or simply is someone who is always thinking of others rather than themselves? Show a carer you care by making them a jacket, hat or scarf – or even the entire warming winter set. Soft alpaca yarn makes the cable knit cosy and luxurious and the classic design means that they will treasure your hard work for many years.

MATERIALS
Yarn
12 [12, 13, 13, 14] 100 g hanks Artesano Aran in C853 Pine

Other Materials
5 buttons

Needles
1 pair 3.75 mm needles
1 pair 5 mm needles
Cable needle

SIZE
Chest: 91 [97, 102, 107, 112] cm (36 [38, 40, 42, 44] ins)

Actual measurement: 102 [107, 112, 119, 124] cm (40 [42, 44, 47, 49] ins)

Length from back neck (excluding collar): 69 [70.5, 71, 71.5, 71.5] cm (27$\frac{1}{4}$ [27$\frac{3}{4}$, 28, 28$\frac{1}{2}$, 28$\frac{1}{4}$] ins).

Sleeve seam: 47 [48, 49.5, 49.5, 51] cm (18$\frac{1}{2}$ [19, 19$\frac{1}{2}$, 19$\frac{1}{2}$, 20] ins)

Figures in square brackets [] refer to the larger sizes. Where only one figure is given this refers to all sizes.

TENSION
25 sts and 24 rows over 10 cm (4 ins) over pattern on 5 mm needles

ABBREVIATIONS
K knit
P purl
Dec decrease(ing)
Inc increase(ing)
St(s) stitch(es)
M1 pick up horizontal loop lying before next stitch and knit into back
Beg beginning
Cont continue
DM double moss stitch
WS wrong side
RS right side
Sl slip
Kb knit into back of
TGS twisted garter stitch (knit into back of every stitch)

GLOSSARY

Tw2r k into front of 2nd st on left needle, then k into 1st st and slip both sts off needle together.

Tw2l k into back of 2nd st on left needle, then k into front of 1st st and slip both sts off needle together.

CB4 slip next 2 sts onto cable needle and leave at back of work, k2 then k 2 sts from cable needle.

CF4 slip next 2 sts onto cable needle and leave at front of work, k2 then k 2 sts from cable needle.

CF3 slip next 2 sts onto cable needle and leave at front of work, p1 then k 2 sts from cable needle.

CB3 slip next st onto cable needle and leave at back of work, k2 then p st from cable needle.

Knitting the Cardigan
Working the Pattern Panel (26 sts)

1st Row: P1, k2, p4 (CF4, p4) twice, k2, p1.

2nd Row: K1, p2, (k4, p4) twice, k4, p2, k1.

3rd Row: P1 (CF3, 92, CB3) 3 times, p1.

4th Row: K2 (p2, k2) 6 times.

5th Row: P2 (CF3, CB3, p2) 3 times.

6th Row: K3 (p4, k4) twice, p4, k3.

7th Row: P3 (CB4, p4) twice, CB4, p3.

8th Row: As 6th row.

9th Row: P2 (CB3, CF3, p2) 3 times.

10th Row: As 4th row.

11th Row: P1 (CB3, p2, CF3) 3 times, p1.

12th Row: As 2nd row.

**Working the Cable Pattern (10 sts):
CF8 or CB8**

1st and 3rd Rows: P1, k8, p1.

2nd and 4th Rows: K1, p8, k1.

5th Row: P1, sl 4 sts onto cable needle and leave at front of work for CF8, and back of work for CB8, k4, then k sts from cable needle.

6th Row: As 2nd row.

7th Row: As 1st row.

8th Row: As 2nd row.

Knitting the Back

Using 3.75 mm needles, cast on 85 [91, 95, 101, 105] sts.

1st Row: K1 * p1, k1, repeat from * to end.

2nd Row: P1 * k1, p1, repeat from * to end.

Repeat last 2 rows until work measures 6 cm (2½ ins), finishing on 1st row.

Inc Row: Rib 3 [4, 5, 6, 5] sts, * m1, rib 2, repeat from * to last 4 [5, 4, 5, 6] sts, m1, rib to end (125 [133, 139, 147, 153] sts).

Change to 5 mm needles.

1st Row: (K1, p1) 2 [4, 4, 4, 5] times, p2, (tw2r, p1) 3 [3, 4, 5, 5] times, CF8 1st row, pattern panel 1st row, CF8 1st row, (k1, p1) 1 [1, 1, 2, 3] times, k1, CB8, pattern panel, CB8, (p1, tw2l) 3 [3, 4, 5, 5] times, p2, (p1, k1) to end of row.

2nd Row: (P1, k1) 2 [4, 4, 4, 5] times, k2, (p2, k1) 3 [3, 4, 5, 5] times, CF8 2nd row, pattern panel 2nd row, CF8 2nd row, (p1, k1) 1 [1, 1, 2, 3] times, p1, CB8, pattern panel, CB8, (k1, p2) 3 [3, 4, 5, 5] times, k2, (k1, p1) to end of row.

3rd Row: (P1, k1) 2 [4, 4, 4, 5] times, p1 (tw2r, p1) 3 [3, 4, 5, 5] times, CF8 3rd row, pattern panel 3rd row, CF8 3rd row, (p1, k1) 1 [1, 1, 2, 3] times, p1, CB8, pattern panel, CB8, (p1, tw2l) 3 [3, 4, 5, 5] times, p2, (k1, p1) to end of row.

4th Row: (K1, p1) 2 [4, 4, 4, 5] times, k2, (p2, k1) 3 [3, 4, 5, 5] times, CF8, pattern panel, CF8, (k1, p1) 1(1, 1, 2, 3) times, k1, CB8, pattern panel, CB8, (k1, p2) 3 [3, 4, 5, 5] times, k2, (p1, k1) to end of row.

These 4 rows form DM at each side and in the middle. Keeping the 26 sts pattern panel and the 10 sts cable panel correct throughout, repeat until work measures 69 [70.5, 71, 71.5, 71.5] cm (27¼ [27¾, 28, 28¼, 28¼] ins) from beg, or desired length.

Shaping the Shoulders

Cast off 41 [44, 47, 49, 51] sts at beg of next 2 rows.

Cast off remaining 43 [45, 45, 49, 51] sts.

Knitting the Left Front

Using 3.75 mm needles, cast on 41 [43, 45, 49, 51] sts.

Work in rib as for back, finishing on 1st row.

Inc Row: Rib 2 [1, 1, 4, 3] sts, m1, rib 2 to last 3 [2, 2, 5, 4] sts, m1, rib to end* (60 [64, 67, 70, 74] sts).

Change to 5 mm needles.

1st Row: (K1, p1) 2 [2, 4, 4, 4, 6] times, p2, (tw2r, p1) 3 times, CF8 1st row, pattern panel 1st row, (p1, tw2r) 2 [2, 3, 4, 4] times, p2, k1.

2nd Row: K3, (p2, k1) 2 [2, 3, 4, 4] times, panel pattern 2nd row, CF8 2nd row, (k1, p2) 3 times, k2, (k1, p1) 2 [4, 4, 4, 6] times.

3rd Row: (P1, k1) 2 [4, 4, 4, 6] times, p2, (tw2r, p1) 3 times, CF8, pattern panel, (p1, tw2r) 2 [2, 3, 4, 4] times, p2, k1.

4th Row: K3, (p2, k1) 2 [2, 3, 4, 4] times, pattern panel, CF8, (k1, p2) 3 times, k2, (p1, k1) 2 [4, 4, 4, 6] times.

These 4 rows form DM at side edge. Keeping 26 sts panel pattern and 10 sts cable correct throughout, repeat until work measures 36 cm (14 ins) from beg, finishing on a WS row.

Shaping the Front Edge

Dec 1 st at end of next and following 4th [4th, 4th, 3rd, 3rd] row until 41 [44, 47, 49, 51] sts remain.

Cont until work measures same as back to shoulder shaping, finishing on same pattern row. Cast off.

Knitting the Right Front

Using 3.75 mm needles, cast on 41 [43, 45, 49, 51] sts.

Work as for Left Front to *.

Change to 5 mm needles.

1st Row: K1, p2, (tw2l, p1) 2 [2, 3, 4, 4] times, panel pattern 1st row, CB8 1st row, (p1, tw2l) 3 times, p2, (p1, k1) to end of row.

2nd Row: (P1, k1) 2 [4, 4, 4, 6] times, k2, (p2, k1) 3 times, CB8 2nd row, pattern panel 2nd row, (k1, p2) 2 [2, 3, 4, 4] times, k3.

3rd Row: K1, p2, (tw2l, p1) 2 [2, 3, 4, 4] times, panel pattern 3rd row, CB8 3rd row, (p1, tw2l) 3 times, p2, (k1, p1) 2 [4, 4, 4, 6] times.

4th Row: (K1, p1) 2 [4, 4, 4, 6] times, k2, (p2, k1) 3 times, CB8 4th row, panel pattern 4th row, (k1, p2) 2 [2, 3, 4, 4] times, k3.

These 4 rows form DM at side edge. Keeping 26 sts panel pattern and 10 sts cable correct throughout, repeat until work measures 36 cm (14 ins) from beg, finishing on a WS row.

Shaping the Front Edge

Dec 1 st at beg of next and every following 4th [4th, 4th, 3rd, 3rd] row until 41 [44, 47, 49, 51] sts remain. Continue until work measures same as back to shoulder shaping.

Cast off.

Knitting the Sleeves (both alike)

Using 3.75 mm needles, cast on 41 [43, 45, 45, 47] sts.

Work in 1x1 rib as for Back until work measures 6 [6, 7.5, 6, 6] cm (2½ [2½, 3, 2½, 2½] ins), finishing on a RS row.

Inc Row: Rib 2 [4, 2, 2, 4] sts, m1, k1. Repeat from * to last 3 [5, 3, 3, 5] sts, m1, rib to end (78 [78, 86, 86, 86] sts). Change to 5 mm needles.

1st Foundation Row: DM 2 [3, 4, 4, 5] sts, p1, CB8 1st row, p1, (k2, p1) 4 times, p1, k2, (p4, k4) twice, p4, k2, p2, (k2, p1) 4 times, p1, CF8 1st row, p1, DM 2 [3, 4, 4, 5] sts.

2nd Foundation Row: DM 2 [3, 4, 4, 5] sts, k1, CF8 2nd row, k1, (k1, p2) 4 times, k2, p2, k4, (p4, k4) twice, p2, k1, (k1, p2) 4 times, k1, CB8 2nd row, k1, DM 2 [3, 4, 4, 5] sts.

1st Row: With RS facing DM 2 [3, 4, 4, 5] sts, p1, CB8 3rd row, p1 (tw2r, p1) 4 times, p1, panel pattern 1st row, p1, (tw2l, p1) 4 times, CF8 3rd row, p1, DM 2 [3, 4, 4, 5] sts.

2nd Row: DM 2 [3, 4, 4, 5] sts, k1, CF8 4th row, k1, (p2, k1) 4 times, k1, pattern panel 2nd row, k1, (p1, k1) 4 times, CB8 4th row, k1, DM 2 [3, 4, 4, 5] sts.

Cont in pattern as set, inc 1st at each end of next and every following 4th row until there are 120 [126, 132, 132, 138] sts. Then cont in pattern until work measures 47 [48, 49.5, 49.5, 51] cm (18½ [19, 19½, 19½, 20] ins) or desired length.

Cast off loosely in pattern.

Finishing
Join shoulder seams.

Knitting the Right Front Band and Collar

Using 3.75 mm needles, cast on 9 sts.

Work in 1x1 rib as for Back until band fits right front to start of neck shaping.

Inc 1 st at end of next and every following alt row until there are 49 [53, 57, 61, 65] sts.

Cont straight until collar measures same as front and back to centre back.

Cast off loosely in rib.

Knitting the Left Front Band and Collar

Using 3.75 mm needles, cast on 9 sts and work 4 rows as for right front band.

1st Buttonhole row: Rib 3, cast off 2 sts, rib to end.

2nd Buttonhole row: Rib 4, cast on 2 sts, rib to end.

Work 16 rows in rib as set.

Repeat last 18 rows 3 more times, and 1st and 2nd rows once.

Cont until work measures same as front to start of collar shaping.

Inc 1st at beg of next and every following alt row until there are 49 [53, 57, 61, 65] sts.

Cont straight until band and collar measures same as right front band and collar.

Cast off loosely in rib.

Finishing
Fold sleeves in half lengthways and join centres to shoulder seams. Sew sleeves in place to back and fronts.

Join side and sleeve seams.

Sew on buttons.

Aran Unisex Hat and Scarf

MATERIALS
Yarn
Hat: 100 g Artesano Aran Alpaca in C853 Pine
Scarf: 300 g Artesano Aran Alpaca in C853 Pine

Needles
1 pair 5 mm needles
1 pair 3.75 mm needles
Cable needle

SIZE
Hat: 43 cm (17 ins)
Scarf: Width:18 cm (7 ins); Length: 173 cm (68 ins) excluding fringe

TENSION
25 sts and 24 rows over 10 cm (4 ins) over pattern on 5 mm needles

ABBREVIATIONS
K knit
P purl
St(s) stitch(es)
RS right side
WS wrong side
K2tog knit two together
P2tog purl two together
M1 pick up horizontal loop from row below and knit into back
TGS or **kb** twisted garter st: knit into back of every stitch
Inc increase(ing)
Dec decrease(ing)

GLOSSARY
1x1 Rib: **1st Row**: *K1, p1, rep from * to last st, k1. **2nd Row**: *P1, k1, rep from * to last st, p1.
Tw2r twist 2 right: knit into 2nd st on needle and then into 1st.
CB6 slip next 3 sts onto cable needle and leave at front of work, knit next 3 sts then knit sts from cable needle.
CB8 slip next 4 sts onto cable needle and leave at front of work, knit next 4 sts then 4 sts from cable needle.
CB4 slip next 2 sts onto cable needle and leave at front of work, knit next 2 sts then knit 2 sts from cable needle.

Knitting the Hat
Using 3.75 mm needles, cast on 111 sts and work in 1x1 rib until work measures 10 cm (4 ins), finishing on a RS row.

Inc Row: Rib 5 (m1, rib 10) to last 6 sts, m1, rib to end (122 sts).

Using 5 mm needles, work as follows:

1st Row: P3 * tw2r, p4, CB8, p4, (tw2r, p4) twice. Repeat from * to end of row, finishing with p3 instead of p4.

2nd Row: Work in pattern.

3rd Row: As 1st row.

4th Row: As 2nd row.

5th Row: P3 * tw2r, p4, CB8, p4 (tw2r, p4) twice. Repeat from * to end of row, finishing with p3 instead of p4.

6th Row: As 2nd row.

7th Row: As 1st row.

8th Row: As 2nd row.

Repeat last row until work measures 19 cm (7½ ins), finishing on 5th row of cable pattern.

Shaping the Crown
Work WS facing.

1st Row: K1, k2tog, (p2, k1, k2tog, k1) twice, p8, * (k1, k2tog, k1, p2) 4 times, p8. Repeat from * to last 9 sts, k1, k2tog, k1, p2, k2tog, k1 (105 sts).

Work 3 rows in pattern.

5th Row: Work as set, dec 2 sts in middle of each cable (97 sts).

Work 3 rows in pattern, substituting CB8 with CB6.

9th Row: K2tog, p2, (k1, k2tog, p2) twice, * p4, (k1, k2tog, p2) 4 times.

Repeat from * to last 10 sts, p4, k1, k2tog, p2, k2tog (80 sts).

Work 1 row.

11th Row: Work as set, dec 2 sts in middle of each cable (72 sts).

Work 3 rows substituting CB6 with CB4.

15th Row: Work as set, dec 2 sts in middle of each cable (64 sts).

Work 3 rows substituting CB4 with tw2r.

19th Row: K1 (p2tog, k2tog) to last 3 sts, p2tog, k1 (33 sts).

Work 3 rows in 1x1 rib.

23rd Row: P2tog to last st, p1 (17sts).

24th Row: K2tog to last st, k1 (9 sts).

25th Row: P2tog to last st, p1 (5 sts).

Finishing
Break yarn, thread through remaining sts and fasten off securely. Join back seam with RS facing to last 5 cm (2 ins). Join remaining seam on RS for brim turn-up.

Knitting the Scarf

Using 5 mm needles, cast on 44 sts.
Work 4 rows in TGS.

Commence Pattern:

1st Row: Kb3 (Tw2r, p2, k6, p2) 3 times,
Tw2r, kb3.

2nd and every alternate row: Kb3
(p2, k2, p6, k2) 3 times, p2, kb3.

3rd Row: Kb3 (Tw2r, p2, CB6, p2) 3
times, Tw2r, kb3.

5th Row: As 1st row.
7th Row: As 1st row.
8th Row: As 2nd row.

Continue in pattern as set until work
measures approx 165 cm (65 ins), approx
56 pattern repeats, ending on a WS row.

Work 4 rows in TGS.

Cast off.

Finishing
Press work. Sew in ends.

Making the Fringes
Cut 14-cm (5½-in) lengths of yarn.
Using 3 pieces together, knot through
every other cast-on and cast-off st.

HINTS AND TIPS

• Don't throw away your ball bands. Keep one to attach to any
left-over yarn so you don't forget what it is. And save others to
give to the recepient along with their knitted garment as the ball
band contains the washing instructions.

• It is a good idea to use a cable needle that is slightly smaller
than the needles you are knitting with as this will ensure that the
stitches don't stretch.

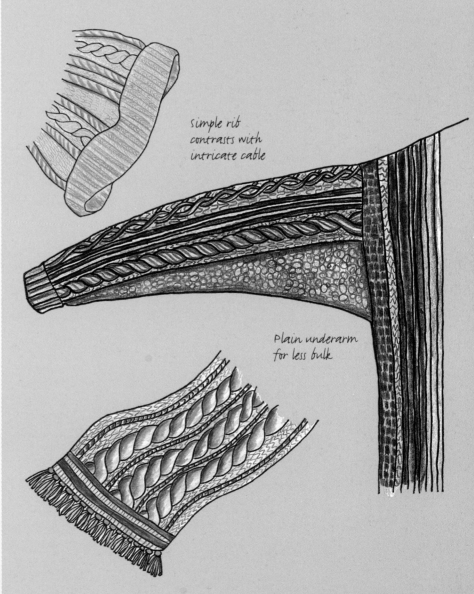

simple rib
contrasts with
intricate cable

Plain underarm
for less bulk

MATERIALS

Yarn
2 skeins Cherry Tree Hill Supersock,
or any gorgeous washable wool yarn
or a decent 4-ply sock yarn

Needles
1 set 3.75 mm double-pointed needles
or 2 x 3.75 mm 40-cm circular needles
Stitch markers
Row counter
Cable needle

SIZE
For a size 10 foot; see pattern for
adjustment instructions for smaller or
larger sizes. You can knit the sock as long
as you need it or the charity requires.

TENSION
20 sts and 30 rows over 6 cm ($2^{1}/_{4}$ in)
over stocking stitch

ABBREVIATIONS
K knit
P purl
St(s) stitch(es)
DPNS double-pointed needles
K2tog knit 2 together
Tbl through the back loop
Dec decrease
Sl slip

GLOSSARY
Kfb k1 st in the front, then in the back
of the same st.
C4F slip next 2 sts onto cable needle
and leave at front of work, k2 then
k2 sts from cable needle.
C4B slip next 2 sts onto cable needle
and leave at back of work, k2 then
k2 sts from cable needle.

SOCKS FOR SOLDIERS
Cable socks for those who serve
by Esther Knight

For the warrior – or the peacemaker – why not knit a smart and comfortable cable sock? This foot-glove is for those who have mastered the simple stocking stitch sock and are ready to have a crack at cables, but perhaps don't have the temperament/time/tranquility in life to embark on a complicated cable such as Eunny Jang's masterpiece, the Beyerische.

Instructions are given for five double-pointed needles, but if you think of them as 4 sections, this works just as well with the magic loop method (see page 93) or my current favourite, two separate 40-cm circular needles (no stretching at the joins and they don't fall out on the train and roll under the seat opposite!). If you are using the latter two techniques, just mark the join where a new double-pointed needle would be with a funky, gorgeous stitch-marker (see page 43); or if you are resourceful, a couple of old safety-pins from the dry cleaners.

KNITTING THE SOCKS

Using the long-tail cast-on method, cast on 64 sts (16 sts per dpn or section).

K2, p2 rib all around until work measures 4.5 cm (1¾ in) – approximately 20 rounds.

To prepare for the cable work in pattern, rearrange your sts so that you start and end with a single p st on each dpn by slipping each end st onto the needle to the left.

If working with magic loops or 2 circular needles, move the markers 1 st to the right so that each section starts and ends with a single p st.

Increase Round: On each dpn/section p1, k2, p2 (kfb twice), p2 (kfb twice), p2, k2, p1 (20 sts per section = 80sts).

Work one round, p all the p st and k all the k sts and all newly created sts. At the end of this round you will still have 80 sts. Set the row counter at 5, as you are about to start Cabling Round 5.

Cabling Round 5: P1, k2, p2, C4F, p2, C4B, p2, k2, p1 on each section (80 sts).

Next 4 Rounds: K all k sts and p all p sts.

Repeat cable round every time the counter shows a multiple of 5; for all other rounds k all the k sts and p all the p sts.

Repeat pattern 10 times.

Sock will measure approx 16-17 cm (6¼–6½ ins), finishing on a round 3.

Decreasing for heel flap
Choose two adjacent sections; these will form the heel flap. The other two sections will form the instep sts. You may wish to mark them so you know which is which.

The following 2 rounds will decrease the 4-st cables in heel flap sections to 2 neat sts which blend in to look like false cables.

1st Round: K2 tog at start of heel area, work in pattern up to the first cable of heel flap, k1, k2tog tbl, k1, p2, k1, k2tog, k1, p2, work in pattern to next section of heel flap and repeat decreases over that

cable pair in the same way, k2tog at end of heel area.

For the instep sts on the rest of the round k all the k sts and p all the p sts as normal.

There should be 40 sts in instep area + 34 sts in heel flap area (74 sts in total).

Next Round: Work in pattern up to the first cable of heel flap area, k1, k2tog tbl, p2, k1, k2tog, work in pattern to next set of cables and repeat.

For the instep sts on the rest of this round, k all the k sts, p all the p sts and work the cables as normal.

There should now be 40 sts in instep area + 30 sts in heel flap area (70 sts in total).

Transfer the instep area to a stitch holder/ loose thread or, if using 2 circular needles, just let the spare one dangle.

Turn and work back over the 30 heel sts, s1, p to end.

Working the Reinforced Heel
Row 1: S1, k1, repeat to end.

Row 2: S1, p to end.

Repeat these 2 rows 12 times, ending with a p row.

Turning the Heel
Row 1: S1, k16, k2tog tbl, k1, turn.
Row 2: S1, p5, p2tog, p1, turn.

Row 3: S1, k6, k2tog tbl, k1, turn.

Row 4: S1, p7, p2tog, p1, turn.

Row 5: S1, k8, k2tog tbl, k1, turn.

Row 6: S1, p9, p2tog, p1, turn.

Row 7: S1, k10, k2tog tbl, k1, turn.

Row 8: S1, p11, p2tog, p1, turn.

Row 9: S1, k12, k2tog tbl, k1, turn.

Row 10: S1, p13, p2tog, p1, turn.

Row 11: S1, k14, k2tog tbl, k1, turn.

Row 12: S1, p15, p2tog, p1 (this should use up all the heel sts), turn.

Row 13: S1, k whole heel (18 sts).

Knitting the Gussets
Round 1: Pick up 16 sts up right side of heel, work in pattern across instep sts on spare needle, pick up and k 16 sts down left side of heel. There should be 40 sts on instep + 50 sts on heel (90 sts).

Round 2: K all k sts and p all p sts, and at heel/instep junction, on heel needle k2 tog tbl, k across sole and up the gusset, at last 2 sts of gusset k2 tog.

The gusset decreases will be next to a single p st on either side of the instep so the join looks the same on both sides.

Continue, knitting plain st st across the sole and cabling every 5th round over the instep.

At the same time, work gusset decreases on alternate rows until there are 30 sts on sole sections and 40 sts on instep.

Continue to work in pattern as set until you are 4 cm (1½ ins) from tip of toe. Unless you have the sock owner's foot easily to hand to try it on at this point, it is useful to have made a cardboard template (see opposite): you need to be about 1 cm (½in) short of the cleft dot), ending on a round 3 of pattern.

Decreasing for the Toecap
Next Round: At the first cable of the instep, k1, k2 tog tbl, k1, p2, k1, k2tog, k1, p2, k2, p2, k2, p2, k1, k2 tog tbl, k1, p2, k1, k2tog, k1, p2, complete round in pattern.

Next Cabling Round: K1, k2 tog tbl, p2, k1, k2 tog, p2, k2, p2, k2, p2, k1, k2 tog tbl, p2, k1, k2 tog, p2 and onward until you meet the sole again (60 sts). Rearrange the sts so that there are 30 on the sole and 30 on the instep and the instep sides are symmetrical.

Knitting the Toecap
Round 1: K1, k2 tog tbl, k across sole to last 3 sts, k2 tog, k1, k1, k2 tog tbl, k across instep to last 3 sts, k2tog, k1.
Round 2: K all round instep and sole. Repeat these 2 rounds until there are 32 sts left, 16 on both instep and sole.

Grafting the Toe (Kitchener Stitch)
Kitchener Stitch is my method of choice (for instructions see Walker's socks, page 93), but this design would work just as well with the inside-out 3-needle cast off.

Finish toes and your sock is complete. Now make sock two.

HINTS AND TIPS

- For a list of charities that collect donations of socks for those serving in the forces, see page 135.

- Next home leave, make a cardboard template by drawing around the recipient's foot and use to check sock length. To work out where to start decreasing for the toecap, put a mark on the card at the cleft of the big toe and its neighbour.

- Here's my Kitchener Stitch aide-memoire: FK off, FP: BP off, BK. Try it for yourself – it works every time!

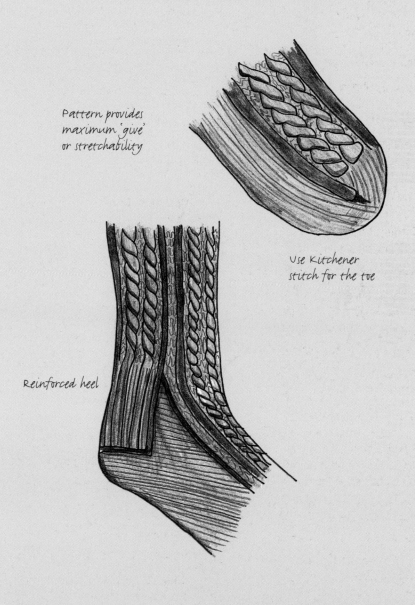

Pattern provides maximum 'give' or stretchability

Use Kitchener stitch for the toe

Reinforced heel

HEARTH & HOME MITTS
Fingerless gloves for an outdoor worker
by Jane Lithgow

These mitts were designed with sellers of the Big Issue in mind as a practical garment that will keep hands warm but leave fingers free for handling papers and money. In fact, they work equally well for gardeners or, indeed, anyone who works outdoors and needs to use their fingers in cold weather. They also remind all outdoor workers of the comforts they will return to at the end of a good day's toil. The brickwork pattern represents the right of everyone to have a home of their own, and the stripes on the thumb, like the bars of a grate, symbolise the need for that home to be warm and safe.

MATERIALS

Yarn
25 g Jamieson's double knitting 100% pure Shetland wool yarn in Crimson (shade 525) (Yarn A)

25 g Jamieson's double knitting 100% pure Shetland wool yarn in Granite (shade 122) (Yarn B)

Other materials
Small amount of waste yarn

Needles
Set of five 3 mm double-pointed needles
2 stitch markers
Blunt tapestry/darning needle

SIZE
To fit an average-sized man's hand

TENSION
5.5 sts and 6 rows over 2.5 cm (1 in) over main pattern

ABBREVIATIONS
K knit
P purl
St(s) stitch(es)
Sl slip
PM place marker
M1 make 1 st
DPNS double-pointed needles

KNITTING THE MITTS

Working the Mitt Body (make two)

Using Yarn A, cast on 48 sts and divide equally onto 4 needles (12 sts per needle).

Join for working in the round.

Work 20 rows in k2 p2 rib.

K 2 rows.

Change to Yarn B without cutting Yarn A.

Row 1: Using Yarn B (k3, k1, wrapping yarn around the needle twice), repeat to end.

Row 2: Using Yarn A (k3, sl1, letting extra loop drop), repeat to end.

Row 3: Using Yarn A (k3, sl1), repeat to end.

Row 4: Using Yarn B, k, k1, wrapping yarn around the needle twice (k3, k1, wrapping yarn around the needle twice) to last 2 sts, k2.

Row 5: Using Yarn A, k1, sl1, letting extra loop drop (k3, sl1, letting extra loop drop) to last 2 sts, k2.

Row 6: Using Yarn B, k1, sl1 (k3, sl1) to last 2 sts, k2.

These 6 rows form the pattern.

Repeat these 6 rows once more.

Knitting the Thumb Gusset

Continuing in pattern, work as follows:

Row 1: Work 24 sts (to end of second needle) pm, m1, work to end of row in pattern.

Row 2: Work in pattern as set (k newly made stitch).

Row 3: Work in pattern to first stitch marker, m1, k1; on 3rd needle, m1, pm, work to end of row.

Repeat Rows 2 and 3, knitting all newly made sts, until there are 15 sts between the markers.

Dividing for the Thumb
Next Row: Work to first marker in established pattern.

Place next 15 sts on a piece of waste yarn, work to end of row.

Continue in pattern until a total of 7 pattern repeats have been worked.

Using Yarn B, k 1 row.

Break off Yarn B.

Using Yarn A, k 2 rows.

Knitting the Finger Border
Work 4 rows in k2 p2 rib.
Cast off reasonably firmly in rib.

Knitting the Thumb Border
Distribute 15 sts from waste yarn onto three dpns.

Join Yarn A and knit one round. At the end of the round pick up and k 1 st from where the thumb joins the palm (16 sts).

Work 3 more rows in k2 p2 rib.

Cast off in rib.

Finishing
Sew in all ends.

HINTS AND TIPS

- Why not use a water-resistant wool such as an unwashed handspun yarn that is full of lanolin? This will stand up better to outdoor conditions and keep hands drier, too.

- If the yarn you want to use is not water-resistant, then there is a special protective product called Nicwax that you can use to treat your finished mitts with.

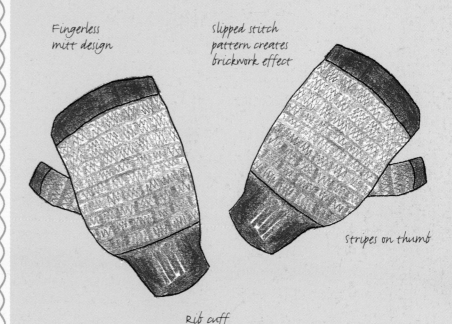

Fingerless mitt design

slipped stitch pattern creates brickwork effect

stripes on thumb

Rib cuff

BAD WEATHER BEANIE
Superfast knit to donate to the homeless
by Gerard Allt

Beginner knitters often ask me for easy hat patterns and this couldn't be much easier. Knitted from the top down, you work through the increases and finish with a straight run. This design would be suitable for anyone. It's super-simple and quick to knit. You can work several up in no time to give to your friends and family. Or why not spend a little time to make a couple for your local charity shop, shelter, day centre or hospice. Thousands of charities rely on donations to pass on to those who are in need.

MATERIALS

Yarn
100 g Silkwood hand-dyed Merino DK

Needles
1 set 3.75 mm double-pointed needles
1 x 3.75 mm 40-cm circular needle

SIZE
To fit an average adult male

TENSION
10 sts and 11 rows over 4 cm (1½ ins)

ABBREVIATIONS

K knit
P purl
Inc increase(ing)
KFB knit in front and back of stitch
DPNS double-pointed needles

KNITTING THE BEANIE

Cast on 6 sts and divide evenly over
3 needles.

1st Round: Knit 1 inc into every stitch.
(12 sts.)

2nd and every alternate Round: Knit.

3rd Round: Inc into every stitch. 24
stitches.

5th Round: K1, (KFB, K3) repeat brackets
until 2 sts remain, K2.

7th Round: K1, (KFB, K4) repeat brackets
until 2 sts remain, K2.

Continue in this manner until the number
of sts between increases is 13, (KFB, K13)
for hat to fit average adult male.

Note: When the number of sts gets too
many to work comfortably with on dpns,
change to the 3.75 mm circular needle.

Knit 40 rounds or to desired length
(see Hints and Tips, right).

Cast off.

HINTS AND TIPS

- Hand-dyed self-striping yarn is fun to use to give interest to
a simple design, however you can substitute any double knit
you have to hand for the yarn used here.

- If possible, try the hat on the recipient before you cast off – if you
decide he needs a longer hat then simply knit a few more rounds.

- Don't want a rolled brim? Then work the last 20 rows in 2x2 rib.

- Why not make a big pom-pom (see page 49) with the extra yarn
and add it to the hat for a little bit of fun!

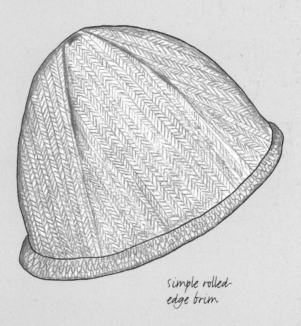

Work from the
crown down

simple rolled
edge brim

BACK PAIN BELT

An easy way to wear a heat or chill pad

by Craig Carruthers

Back pain is very prevalent and soothing heat or chill pads can be an effective way to treat the symptoms, but the belts available to use with the pads are often made from uncomfortable and ugly synthetic fabric. Why not knit a softer, sexier version from a good-quality yarn? When you are not there to massage an aching back this is a touching way to cherish a loved one.

MATERIALS

Yarn
100 g Silkwood hand-dyed Double Knit

Needles
1 pair 3.5 mm needles

Other Materials
2 buttons

SIZE
To fit a 86 cm (34 in) waist. Adjust position of button to fit

TENSION
14 sts and 10 rows over 4 cm (1½ in)

ABBREVIATIONS
K knit
P purl
Inc increase
St(s) stitch(es)
Fwd forward
Tog together

KNITTING THE BELT

Cast on 12 sts.

Work in moss stitch as follows:

1st Row: K1, p1 to end.

2nd Row: P1, k1 to end.

Repeat these 2 rows until work measures 28 cm (11 ins).

Inc 1 st at each end of every following 3rd row until there are 42 sts.

Cast on 28 sts at beginning of next 2 rows, keeping moss stitch pattern (98 sts).

Continue in moss stitch on these 98 sts until work measures 20 cm (8 ins) from cast-on row.

Cast off 28 sts at beginning of next 2 rows (42 sts).

Dec 1 st at each end of next and every following 3rd row until 12 sts remain.

Continue in moss stitch on these 12 sts for 19 cm (7½ ins).

Working the buttonhole
Make buttonhole in the next row that commences with a purl st: work 5 sts, yarn fwd, work 2tog, work to end of row.

Work another 5 cm (2 ins) in moss stitch.

Make another buttonhole as before.

Work a further 4 cm (1½ ins) in moss stitch.

Cast off.

Finishing
Turn in flaps and stitch to form a centre pocket with overlapping opening.

Sew on button to suit waist measurement.

HINTS AND TIPS
- Women will find the belt useful too – and not just for back pain. By wearing the pouch at the front, it aids stomach aches and cramps.

- If you don't want a button and buttonhole closure, omit the working and continue the pattern in moss stitch. Then add touch-and-close fastening at the finishing stage instead.

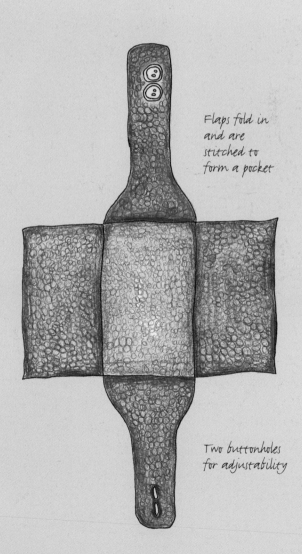

Flaps fold in and are stitched to form a pocket

Two buttonholes for adjustability

Bringing Care Home

A POSITIVE PILLOW TO BRING GOOD MESSAGES

Stitches that spell out care

FUNDRAISING TEA COSY

Bring cheer to any event

ECO-FRIENDLY TOTE BAG

A plastic carrier with the Earth at heart

A POSITIVE PILLOW TO BRING GOOD MESSAGES
Stitches that spell out care
by Celia Reynolds

Why not make this beautifully soft pillow for someone who needs a little tender loving care? Celia, who works in my store, thought so, and came in to work one morning with this positive contribution to the book.

There is a chart with the entire alphabet provided overleaf, so you can customize Celia's design to spell out an appropriate message for the recipient you have in mind. The softest wool and a border design that includes hearts reinforces your loving words. Celia chose an oblong shape as it makes the pillow more huggable.

MATERIALS

Yarn
400 g Rowan Cocoon Polar (Yarn A)

400 g Rowan Cocoon Scree (Yarn B)

25 g Rowan Kidsilk Haze in shade 606
(Yarn C)

Needles
1 pair 7 mm needles

SIZE
57 cm (22½ ins) X 35.5 cm (14 ins)

TENSION
18 sts and 25 rows over 10 cm (4 ins)
over stocking stitch

ABBREVIATIONS
K knit

P purl

St(s) stitch(es)

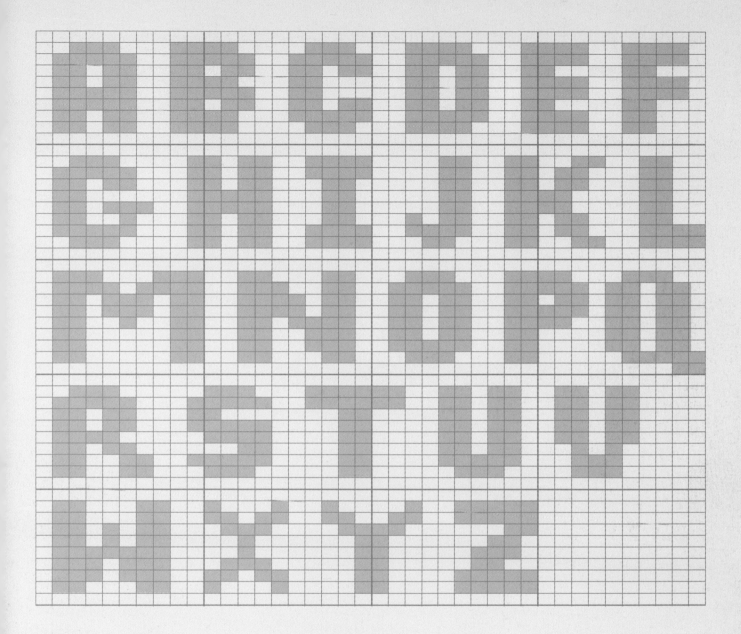

It is important to plot out your pillow message on squared paper or in a computer program designed for the purpose and check that it will fit in the panel. If you want a longer or shorter panel you will have to adjust the length of the central panel and borders. Check out www.knitonthenet.com for advice and templates for charting.

KEY

Background colour

Accent colour

Work in stitches of your choice.

KNITTING THE PILLOW

Knitting the Front

Using Yarn A, cast on 100 sts.

1st Row: K1 (k1, p1) 5 times, place marker, (p1, k5) 4 times, p1, k1, place marker, (k1, p1) 13 times, place marker, (p1, k5) 4 times, p1, k1, place marker, (p1, k1) 5 times, k1.

(The markers help delineate the sections of varying stitches.)

2nd Row: K1 (k1, p1) 5 times, p2 (k1, p3, k1, p1) 4 times, (p1, k1) 13 times, p2 (k1, p3, k1, p1) 4 times, (p1, k1) 5 times, k1.

3rd Row: K1 (k1, p1) 5 times, k2 (p1, k1, p1, k3) 4 times, (k1, p1) 13 times, k2 (p1, k1, p1, k3) 4 times, (p1, k1) 5 times, k1.

4th Row: K1 (k1, p10) 5 times, p4 (k1, p5) 3 times, k1, p3 (p1, k1) 13 times, p4 (k1, p5) 3 times, k1, p3 (p1, k1) 5 times, k1.

Repeat these 4 rows twice more.

13th Row: K11, using a single strand of Yarn A plus 2 strands of Yarn C together, k next 78 sts, using Yarn A only, k11.

The centre panel of 78 sts is worked throughout with 3 strands as above, while the 11 sts forming the borders should be continued in Yarn A only.

14th Row: K1, p4, k1, p5, p78, p5, k1, p4, k1.

15th Row: K4, p3, k4, k78, k4, p3, k4.

16th Row: K1, p2, k5, p3, p78, p3, k5, p2, k1.

17th Row: K3, p5, k3, k78, k3, p5, k3.

18th Row: K1, p1, k7, p2, k78, p2, k7, p1, k1.

19th Row: K2, p7, k2, k78, k2, p7, k2.

20th Row: As 18th Row.

21st Row: As 19th Row.

22nd Row: K1, p2, k5, p3, p78, p3, k5, p2, k1.

23rd Row: K3, p2, k1, p2, k3, k78, k3, p2, k1, p2, k3.

24th Row: K1, p2, k2, p1, k2, p3, k78, p3, k2, p1, k2, p2, k1.

25th Row: K11, k78, k11.

26th Row: K1, p10, p78, p10, k1.

27th Row: K1 (k1, p1) 5 times. For centre 78 sts, follow chart on page 125, using Yarn B for lettering, (p1, k1) 5 times, k1.

28th Row: K1 (k1, p1) 5 times, k78 as chart, (p1, k1) 5 times, k1.

29th to 48th Rows: Follow chart over centre 78 sts, continuing to work borders in moss stitch.

49th to 54th Rows: Continue moss stitch borders, working centre 78 sts in stocking stitch.

55th to 66th Rows: As Rows 13 to 26.

67th Row: Using Yarn A only (which will be used until pillow is completed), k.

68th Row: P.

69th to 80th Rows: As rows 1 to 12. Cast off.

Back

Using Yarn A, cast on 100 sts.

Work in moss stitch as follows:

1st Row: K1, p to last 2 sts, k2.

2nd Row: K2 (p1, k1) to end.

Repeat these 2 rows until back measures same as front.

Cast off.

Finishing

Press according to instructions on yarn band.

With right sides facing, join the 2 pieces together, leaving a gap for turning and stuffing.

Stuff as required and slipstitch gap closed.

HINTS AND TIPS

- To choose your colours, place a ball of the lettering colour on top of a pile of balls of the ground shade you have selected for the central panel of the pillow. Stand back and see if the lettering colour is strong enough to stand out.

- If you are not sure how to knit lettering, be sure to consult reputable knitting instruction books before you start.

- The design is adaptable: if you want a shorter pillow just reduce the number of stitches you work in the central panel. To simplify the design you could work the entire border in moss stitch.

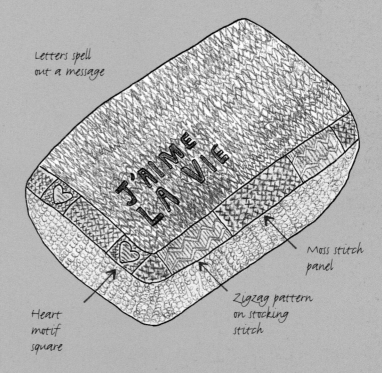

Letters spell out a message

Heart motif square

Zigzag pattern on stocking stitch

Moss stitch panel

FUNDRAISING TEA COSY
Bring cheer to any event
by Amanda Perkins

Tea cosies are all the rage again. They make a great gift and are perfect to knit for sale at a charity fundraiser. You can use them at your tea stall, too, to promote your wares! The yarns suggested here make a luxuriously soft and warm cosy for that special present for a tea-loving friend or relative. If you are making the cosy for charity and you want to minimize the expense and maximize the revenue, then you can substitute yarns (see page 138 for advice on this). Why not buy a jolly assortment of odd balls from a charity store and double the fundraising revenues the cosy generates?

MATERIALS
50 g Natural Dye Studio's Baby Alpaca/ Merino Chunky, rolled into 2 balls (Yarn A)

30 g Natural Dye Studio's Merino Chunky Loop, rolled into 2 balls (Yarn B)

NEEDLES
1 pair 6 mm needles

TENSION
4 sts and 5 rows over 4 cm (1½ ins)

ABBREVIATIONS
K knit

P purl

St(s) stitch(es)

Tog together

Knitting The Tea Cosy
Using Yarn A, cast on 51 sts.

Rows 1 – 4: K1, p1 rib.

Row 5: K.

Row 6: P.

Working the Spout Hole
Row 7: K24, cast off 3 sts, k to end.

Row 8: Still using Yarn A, k24, using Yarn B k remaining 24 sts.

Row 9 (bobble row): ***K3, *using Yarn B k5, turn, k4, turn, k3, turn, k2, turn, k1, turn, k2, turn, k3, turn, K4, turn, using Yarns A and B together k5, using Yarn A k3.

Repeat from * twice. **

Break off Yarn B.

Repeat from *** to ** for the second half of row 9 using Yarn A.

Row 10: P.

Row 11: K.

Row 12: P.

Row 13 (bobble row): K6, * using Yarn B k5, turn, k4, turn, k3, turn, k2, turn, k1, turn, k2, k3, turn, k4, turn, using Yarns B and A together k5, using Yarn A k3.

Repeat from *, k6.

Row 14: P.

Row 15: K.

Row 16: P.

Row 17 (bobble row): Repeat Row 9.

Row 18: P23, p2 tog (sts linking left and right section), p23 (47 sts).

Knitting the Tea Cosy Top

Row 19: K.

Row 20: P5, p2 tog; repeat to end of row (41 sts).

Row 21 (bobble row): *Using Yarn B k5, turn, k4, turn, k3, turn, k2, turn, k1, turn, k2, k3, turn, k4, turn, using Yarns B and A together k5, using Yarn A k3.

Repeat from * five times.

Row 22: P4, p2 tog, repeat to last st, p1 (35 sts).

Row 23: K.

Row 24: P3, p2 tog, repeat to end of row (28 sts).

Row 25 (bobble row): K2, *using yarn B k3, turn, k2, turn, k1, turn, k2, turn, using Yarns B and A together k3, using Yarn A k2.

Repeat from * five times, but as there are not enough sts left for 2 between each bobble, k1 after bobbles 1, 3 and 5.

Row 26: P2, p2 tog, repeat to end of row (21 sts).

Row 25: K.

Row 26: . P1, k2 tog, repeat to end of row (14 sts).

Break off yarn, leaving a 25-cm (10-in) length for sewing up cosy. Thread yarn through remaining 14 sts and pull tight.

Finishing

Sew up seam, leaving enough space for your teapot handle to fit through.

HINTS AND TIPS

- If you omit the 3-stitch cast off in the middle of row 7 and knit those stitches, too, and then sew up the entire seam when you are finishing the piece, voila: a mad bobble hat!

- Get creative with colour combinations: knit a white version with red bobbles for a Christmas present or fundraising event, a pale pink one with deep pink bobbles for a breast cancer charity fundraiser, or one in club colours for a team event.

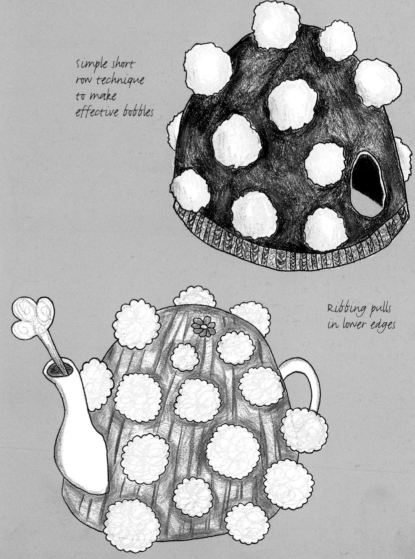

simple short row technique to make effective bobbles

Ribbing pulls in lower edges

MATERIALS

Yarn

Approximately 44 standard carrier bags cut into strips 3 cm (1¼ ins) wide, plus extra for pockets

Needles

1 pair 5 mm needles

Other Materials

2 plastic hoops for handles

SIZE

The bag measures 40 cm (16 ins) across and 45 cm (18 ins) long

TENSION

20 sts and 32 rows over 10 cm (4 ins) over garter stitch on 5 mm needles

ABBREVIATIONS

K knit

P purl

St(s) stitch(es)

KNITTING THE TOTE

Cast on 80 st and work in garter stitch until work measures 88 cm (34½ ins).

Next row: K 5, turn and continue in garter stitch for 15 rows on these 5 sts. Cast off.

Rejoin plastic to remaining 75 sts and cast off the next 5 st, k 5 and turn. K 15 rows on these 5 sts as before. Continue in this way until there are no more stitches left. This creates one set of tabs to fasten over the handles.

To work the other set, turn the work upside down and pick up 5 sts at the beginning of the cast-on edge and work 15 rows in garter stitch.

ECO-FRIENDLY TOTE BAG
A plastic carrier with the Earth at heart
by Emily Blades

Be Green and Get Seen! Now you can indulge your handbag addiction while feeling good about doing your bit to save the planet, recycling all those unwanted plastic bags.

This stylish and unique tote can be used for any occasion. Whether on the beach, carrying your knitting, or just making a fashion statement, it is sure to be an attention-grabber.

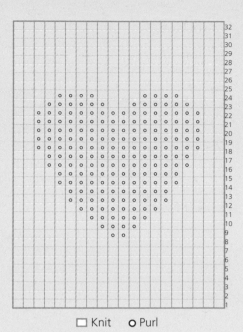

☐ Knit   ○ Purl

Cast off.

Leave a gap of 5 sts and pick up a further 5 sts, k 15 rows and cast off.

Continue in this way until all the tabs have been worked.

Pockets (make 9)
These are worked in stocking stitch. Cast on 20 sts and work 32 rows, incorporating your choice of picture design (see Hints and Tips). Cast off.

Finishing
Fold the work in half and sew up the sides, using the remainder of the plastic yarn. (Having no seam at the bottom makes the bag stronger.)

Space the pockets evenly onto the front of the bag and stitch into place, remembering to leave the tops open!

Fold and stitch each tab over the handles.

HINTS AND TIPS

- You don't have to knit hearts into the pockets; you can decorate the pockets with your choice of picture pattern. These can be designed using special knitting graph paper or chosen ready-made from good knitting books. The end result is impressive whichever method you choose.

- This design is large enough to take all your shopping or beach gear. If you want a shallower tote to use as a handbag, simply knit fewer rows.

- Only use carriers you have accumulated; asking stores for extras to complete your project defeats the purpose!

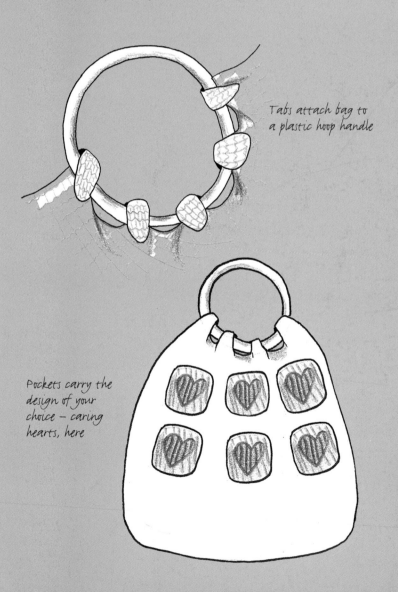

Tabs attach bag to a plastic hoop handle

Pockets carry the design of your choice – caring hearts, here

Appendix

KNITTING FOR CHARITY

One of the most satisfying things that I can do, as a knitter, is knit for charity. Working on Knit A River (see pages 12-13) was incredibly rewarding and I love the fact that I can spend just a couple of pounds on yarn and a couple of hours of time to make a hat for child who needs it more than me. Simple actions can have profound results. We all have the power to help people in need. A hat for an orphaned child, a blanket for disaster-relief appeals, socks for soldiers, gloves for the homeless… the list is endless. (See www.dailyknitter.com for a list of charities you can knit for.)

Useful Addresses

KNITTING FOR BABIES

Early Angels Project

Blankets and baby clothes for premature, low birthweight and still-born babies.

www.geocities.com/earlyangelsproject

Bonnie Babies

Blankets, cardigans and bonnets for premature, low birthweight and still-born babies.

www.bonniebabies.co.uk

Ray of Hope

Bonnets, cardigans, bootees, blankets, mitts for premature babies. Includes knitting for Christmas parcels.

www.rayofhope.co.uk

Bliss

Knitted boobs to help new mums with sick or premature babies learn to express their milk.

www.bliss.org.uk

Little Love

Blankets, bonnets, beanies for premature, miscarried or still-born babies.

http://beehive.courier.co.uk

Loving Hands

Knitting for premature babies (alongside the Linda McDonald Foundation).

www.lovinghands.org.uk

Baby Pack Project

Blankets, cardigans and clothing or baby items for baby-care packs for disadvantaged mothers.

www.freewebs.com/babypackproject

Save the Children

Hats for newborn babies, ill, premature or born into poverty.

www.savethechildren.org.uk

THE HOMELESS

Salvation Army

Knit and natter club, sweaters, teddy bears and any knitwear for the homeless or disadvantaged.

www2.salvationarmy.org.uk

Cubs for Kids

Bears for homeless children across America.

www.cubsforkids.com

ORPHANS

Road (Romanian Aid Distribution)

Blankets, jumpers, hats, scarves and mittens for Romanian orphans.

www.romaid.org.uk

POVERTY

Baby Bear Project

Baby clothes and blankets for the poorest families in South Africa, particularly those suffering from AIDS.

www.babybearproject.tk

Algerian Action

Clothing and toys for needy babies and children in Algeria.

www.algerianaction.co.uk

Blankets for the Gulf

Blankets for hurricane victims.

www.blanketsforthegulf.com

Teddies for Tragedies

Teddies for needy children.

www.teddiesfortragedies.org.uk

Feed The Children

Blankets, jumpers, clothes for children in poverty.

www.feedthechildren.org.uk

Samaritan's Purse

Knitted glove puppets for victims, particularly children, of war poverty, famine, disease and natural disaster.

www.samaritanspurse.uk

Facilitaid

Making and selling knitted teddies for schools in Burundi.

www.facilitaid.com

CSV

Knitting bears for children in distress.

www.csv.org.uk

CSV – Retired and Senior Volunteer Programme

Knitting volunteers make a variety of goods for worthwhile causes, mainly clothing for premature babies, trauma teddies for children in distress and other items of clothing for those in need, wherever they may be.

www.csv-rsvp.org.uk

Knitting for Kisiizi

Relieving poverty by sending clothing, blankets and bedding to Kisiizi Hospital in Uganda.

www.offingtonpark.com

SEAFARERS/SOLDIERS

Sock Knitters

Socks for troops and the people of Afghanistan.

www.socknitters.com

British and International Sailor's Society

Knitting woolly hats for sailors.

www2.biss.org.uk

Poppy Appeal

Knitted poppies for Remembrance Day, in association with The Royal British Legion.

www.knitonthenet.com/poppies

CANCER PATIENTS

Caps for a Cure

Hats for chemotherapy patients.

www.groups.yahoo.com/group/capsforacure

Chemo Caps

Caps for chemotherapy patients.

www.chemocaps.com

PETS IN NEED

K9 Knitters

Knitting dog coats for dog shelters.

www.k9knitters.co.uk

Loving Hands

Blankets for animal shelters.

www.lovinghands.org.uk

FOR THE ELDERLY

The Big Knit with Innocent Drinks

Knitting small hats for Innocent drinks bottles to raise money for Age Concern, to help keep older people warm in winter.

www.innocentdrinks.co.uk/thebigknit

Loving Hands

Work with Blythswood, caring for the elderly in Eastern European countries. www.lovinghands.org.uk

OECS Operation Elderly Charity stitchers

Lap quilts and blankets for elderly residents in nursing homes.

www.uk.geocities.com/oecs_central

Friends to Seniors

Lap quilts and blankets for elderly residents in nursing homes or alone in the UK or US.

www.friends2seniors.com

Threads of Compassion

Scarves for victims of sexual violence.

www.threadsofcompassion.bravehost.com

GENERAL

Little Lamb Charity Blanket Project

Squares for blankets to send to anyone who may need the warmth of a blanket.

www.littlelambblanketproject.squarespace.com

Pompom International

Promotes peace through pompom-making.

www.pompominternational.com

KNITTING FOR WELL-BEING

Knitting has benefits that go much further than simply occupying you with an enjoyable hobby. As you knit, rhythmically winding the yarn around your needles and creating the different stitches, you will experience a satisfying repetition in which your mind switches off from everyday cares and concerns and wanders where it wants, periodically being brought back to the activity of knitting; very much like a meditation. You will soon find that knitting allows you to become more relaxed and calm and able to concentrate better generally. This means that knitting is a healing tool, which can help general anxiety and a number of behavioural conditions. It can even be used as part of a pain-management programme.

Healing through knitting

I'm passionate about knitting and it means everything to me: it is a vital creative skill, allowing me to make useful things and it's an incredibly enjoyable, soothing activity. However, I've discovered that knitting has its more serious side. It allows us to make something for another person, which is very satisfying in itself, and it can also help us to heal ourselves, which is an amazing thought! My friend Betsan Corkhill, of Stitchlinks*, has done a lot of research on how the activity of knitting can affect us, the way it can heal us and even help us to manage medical conditions. She describes it in this way:

'Research has shown that giving to charity stimulates the brain's 'reward centre', which releases powerful feelgood chemicals. Knitting encourages sharing and giving, enabling you to experience a sense of belonging, which is important for well-being and happiness. It can be used as an effective, portable tool to build resilience and develop coping skills to deal with medical conditions such as pain, depression and stress as well as life's normal lows. The rhythmic, repetitive movement, distraction and sensory input combine to give you a powerful coping tool for life, whilst the induced meditative state promotes relaxation. Each completed row and project gives a sense of accomplishment, boosting self-esteem and confidence, giving you control. Sharing this experience with others enhances the benefits, helping to forge firm, lasting friendships. Caring, sharing and giving are vital for building strong relationships and communities – knitting facilitates this, filling lives with colour.'

 * Stitchlinks is an organization encouraging people to knit in order to help heal themselves – whether from isolation or illness. Visit www.stitchlinks.com.

Community knitting groups

Knitters can offer to share their skills and so help improve the wellbeing and quality of life for others. Knitting is a very sociable activity as it lets you talk while you work and this might give you an opportunity to help those who are marginalized or isolated. A knitting group gives everyone a reason to get together with others, on a regular basis, and it can even help them become more empowered socially – as well as improving their knitting skills, of course! If you have the time and inclination, maybe you can volunteer to run a class for patients at your local hospital, or perhaps you could start up 'stitch and bitch' community group in the area where you live.

CHOOSING YARN

When you walk into the Aladdin's cave of your local yarn shop and are mesmerized by the enticing selection of yarns – thin and thick, smooth and fluffy, bright and subtle – you know you are itching to start knitting something, but where do you start? Your chosen pattern will give you precise requirements as to yarn weight (4-ply, double-knitting, Aran, chunky or extra-bulky) and type (wool, mohair, cashmere, alpaca, angora, cotton, linen or acrylic). The choice of colour is, of course, up to you.

Substituting yarns

Every now and then you'll see a yarn that you really want to use, but it isn't the one recommended in the pattern. Alternatively, you may already have a pattern, but be unable to find the specified yarn. Or you may have some ends of balls you want to use, or even some ripped-out (unravelled) yarn you are dying to knit up into something new. The good news is that it's really not that difficult to substitute yarns, but here are some useful hints and tips to help you on your way.

First, the tension of the pattern is key; the number of stitches and rows per inch in the original pattern. This means you can find a yarn that creates the same tension to make that pattern (look for the tension guide on the yarn ball band). If the tension is not included in the pattern, what is the weight of the yarn (is it chunky, worsted or fingering?). Try knitting a sample square. If the tension doesn't match, change the size of your needles. For too-tight tension try larger needles; for too-loose tension try smaller needles.

Yarns and allergies

What can you do when you finally put on your latest creation – the product of hours of hard knitting – only to find that your eyes start to water, you start sneezing or your skin starts to itch uncontrollably? You are probably allergic to wool, or it could be the dye, or even the washing powder you used on it. What are your options? You need to choose your knitting yarn carefully, as allergies can be caused by

acrylics, the lanolin in wool and the dust the wool attracts. However, don't be discouraged: although we all have the potential to be allergic to anything, the following yarns are more likely to be allergy-free than others and are well worth trying out as an alternative to the main culprit: wool.

Alternatives to wool yarn:

Acrylic yarns	Linen	Silk
Alpaca	Lycra	Soy
Bamboo	Nylon	Tencel
Cotton	Polyester	Viscose yarns
Hemp	Rayon	
Ingeo		

See: *No Sheep for You*, Amy Singer, Interweave Press, for an in-depth survey on allergy-free yarns and loads of ideas and patterns for good things to knit.

See the following pages for patterns that use allergy-friendly yarns:

Pages 24-27 Baby's Coming Home
(uses Rowan Fine Milk Cotton)

Pages 38-43 Scratch-free Sweater
(uses Pure Superfine Alpaca)

Pages 50-51 Red-Hot Chilli Scarf
(Double-Knit Alpaca)

Pages 66-71 To Maternity and Beyond
(Knit One Crochet Too Babyboo – bamboo/nylon mix)

Making yarn from plastic bags

Using up plastic bags to make yarn to knit with is a feel-good activity on two levels. It's not only a great way to create a pleasing, soft and highly usable yarn but also a perfect opprtunity to recycle all those bags that seem to be breeding in your kitchen drawer and which you never find another use for. The best types of bag to use for yarn are the thinnest ones, with handles, usually used to tote your fruit and veggies. They are generally plain in colour and unprinted, coming in a range of tasteful whites, greys, blues and greens. If you ever find pinks, reds or oranges, do hang on to them – they're a rare breed and you'll need them to liven up your knitting colour scheme. The next thing to do is to wash the bags and then make sure they're really dry. Now cut them into strips, following the instructions below. You can join them all up to make a continuous double-stranded yarn by knotting loops together before winding them into a ball. Now you're ready to get knitting!

To make the plastic-bag yarn

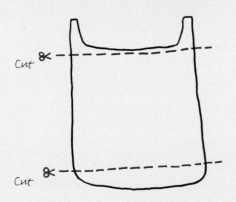

1. Flatten out the bag as smoothly as you can. Cut the top, including handles, off. Cut the bottom of the bag off.

Turn the bag 90°

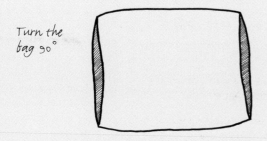

2. Turn the bag through 90 degrees, so that the openings are at the sides.

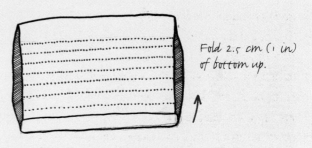

Fold 2.5 cm (1 in) of bottom up.

3. Fold from the bottom, leaving around 5 cm (2 ins) free at the top.

IMPORTANT: Leave at least 5 cm (2 in) of unfolded bag at top

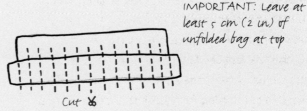

4. Cut the strips to the desired width, leaving at least 2.5 cm (1 in) uncut at the top.

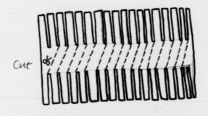

5. Open out the whole bag before completing the cutting on the diagonal, as shown, to create a continuous strip..

Index

Acknowledgements

Gerard Allt would like to thank:

All the designers – Emily Blades, Craig Carruthers, Heather Dixon, Eirwen Godfrey, Sue Hanmore, Sue Hawkins, Julia Hopson, Just Call Me Ruby, Esther Knight, Jane Lithgow, Judith More, Amanda Perkins, Julie Prior, Celia Reynolds, Susan Ryder, Melissa Williams, and Judith Wright.

I would also like to thank all the I Knit Londoners. I've met so many amazing people and made so many brilliant friends that I really can't imagine life without I Knit London.It would be impossible to thank you all individually, but honestly, without you there would not be I Knit London.

Thanks must surely go to Vicky and Philip and Maxine and Jimmy because Louis and James are brilliant!

Thank you, also, to Craig. I love you. Without you I'm just knitting.

Fil Rouge Press would like to thank:

Sharon Spencer for her patience, Robin Lever for his good humour and all the rest of the team for their hard work!

Thanks, too, to the models:
The three charming children and their parents; the adult models: Alex Beale; Philip Cashman; Patricia Bueno Delgado; Naomi Elliot; Lily More; Elizabeth Raus; Nathan Vaughan Harris; Elkie Corcoran; Nicole Cilian.

Finally, but not least of all, Lou Suggs for her immaculate and immediate knitting skills and all the yarn companies who generously donated yarns for the projects.

All photographs by Robin Lever except for pages 13 and 15. Page 13: Gerard Allt, Craig Carruthers, Steve Bainbridge. Page 15: Gerard Allt, Craig Carruthers.